GREAT FALLS I'VE TAKEN

To Karen,
Catherine Raggy
4/29/25

GREAT FALLS I'VE TAKEN

A Memoir *of* Disability Layered
with Love *and* Happiness

CATHERINE RAGGIO

LUMINARE PRESS
WWW.LUMINAREPRESS.COM

Great Falls I've Taken: A Memoir of Disability Layered with Love and Happiness
Copyright © 2023 by Catherine Raggio

All rights reserved. This book or any portion thereof may not be reproduced or used in any manner whatsoever without the express written permission of the publisher, except for the use of brief quotations in a book review.

Printed in the United States of America

Cover design by Nina Leis
Author photo by Lawrence Roffee
Cover photo: The author, age three and a half, is pictured one year after having polio.

Luminare Press
442 Charnelton St.
Eugene, OR 97401
www.luminarepress.com

LCCN: 2023913947
ISBN: 979-8-88679-351-2

My memoir is dedicated to my husband, Jim Raggio, the most enlightened and sensitive man I've ever known. With endless patience and tremendous kindness, he believes in me and has constantly encouraged me to pursue my dreams. He also comforts me when I become discouraged and when I have a "great fall." Without his support, my memoir would have remained a series of private, cathartic works occasionally typed out fast and furiously.

CONTENTS

Introduction 1

Part 1
TRAUMA AND RECOVERY

Traumatized 7
Hard Knock Life 10
Surviving Alone 14
Strong Families Build Resilient Kids 19
In Search of…Role Models 26
Moving to the 'Burbs 30
My Defining Year 34
The Splinter 44

Part 2
ADOLESCENCE IS NOT FOR THE FAINT HEARTED

Fitting In Again 49
Coming to Grips with Reality 52
Undies 54
Teen Angst 59
John Derrico, I Forgive You 65
The Driving Lesson 67

Queen of the Prom 72
Discrimination 101—An Introductory Course 76
Off to College 80

Part 3
FINDING MY NICHE IN THIS WORLD

Launching My Career 89
Discovering My Purpose 96
Times Were Changing 102
My Destiny 107
The Beginning of My Best Life 111
Olé 114

Part 4
ON A MISSION

Such a Good Use of Our Tax Dollars! 123
The Press Conference 132
Airborne! 135
And Then We Were Four 138
No One Ever Patted My Tummy (Thankfully) ... 145
An Interval as a Stay-At-Home Mom 148
Spunky 153
A Night in Left Field 157
People on the Go 161

A Nonprofit Entrepreneur ... 170
INnovation at IN ... 175
Happy Hours in Nursing Homes? ... 178
Youth Is Definitely Not Wasted on the Young! ... 180
If My Parents Could See Me Now ... 183
No Sirens, Please! ... 195
Grandchildren Are the Best! ... 198

Part 5
REFLECTIONS

My Mother ... 203
A Pat on the Head and Other Stereotypical Transgressions ... 205
What's Your Comfort Level? ... 208
An Awesome Life ... 212
Murphy's Laws of Falling ... 215

Acknowledgements ... 217

Introduction

I had polio in 1950, shortly before my third birthday. I was fitted with a steel leg brace and relearned how to walk with crutches, but my leg, back, and abdominal muscles remained quite weak. So, I fell . . . often; hence, the title for this book. Being disabled meant that many of the experiences on my life's journey would be different from those of my peers. The bumps in the road I encountered could have altered my vision for my future, but I was determined to set my own course and realize the American dream.

There are two categories of "bumps in the road." One set is caused by the disability itself, such as my frequent falling. Less predictable, however, are the bumps in the second category, such as the attitudes of others, often complete strangers, toward my disability. These attitudinal barriers are experienced by many of us with disabilities. They are part of the foundation of disability culture.

Many of the attitudinal barriers are the result of stereotypes about disability. In my essay, *A Pat on the Head and Other Stereotypical Transgressions*, I touch on some common stereotypes with real-life examples. I would like to think that our society is much more enlightened now than when the incidents I cite happened, but my fear is that the stereotypes persist covertly now in people's minds.

Navigating a world without knowing where or when an attitudinal barrier may occur is taxing. Include experiences caused by our disabilities, such as the many falls I have taken, and you begin to see how daunting it is to succeed.

Falling can take many forms. Mostly, I hit the ground and needed to scrape my disability pride off the pavement. Other times I endured a personal failure or was thwarted by either blatant or subtle discrimination. I began by writing essays about falling, which proved to be cathartic. My pent-up humiliation borne of hundreds of falls, often in public before "God and 1,000 witnesses," was expressed sometimes with humor and sarcasm and occasionally through tears. Writing, I discovered, was liberating, far cheaper than therapy, and healthier than medication. More recently, I wove a narrative of my life story around these essays, thus creating this memoir.

In many ways, nothing about my life is exciting or noteworthy, because my goal was to have a typical life, and I achieved that goal. Realizing the American Dream could never have been presumed, though. The outcomes and rewards have exceeded my expectations. However, I am acutely aware my life could have taken different turns, producing unfulfilling results. Because my life is a gift for which I am incredibly grateful, I invest my time in ventures that help others succeed as they find their way to success and a satisfying life.

PART 1

TRAUMA AND RECOVERY

1

Traumatized

My first memory of life is thrashing about and screaming in a hospital cubicle as two nurses laid something heavy across my legs. Sandbags. The nurses sought to immobilize me to prevent paralysis. Being a month shy of my third birthday and without the comfort of my parents or my baby doll named Janie, who was confiscated due to her exposure to the polio virus, I fought mightily to free myself from these bonds.

A similar scene undoubtedly was played out in hospitals across the country as my parents and I joined thousands of other families in the early 1950s who were suddenly visited by the polio virus. My devoted parents, along with countless others in the same situation, wore masks and took up residence in the lobby or paced the halls of the hospital but were not allowed to enter the polio ward due to fear of contagion. It was the summer of 1950, and polio had reached epidemic proportions in the greater Pittsburgh area where I lived.

My mother accompanied me in the ambulance to the hospital where I was diagnosed with polio and admitted. Her pain at learning I had polio and leaving me alone at the hospital was almost unbearable. Further, her only option for getting back home after my hospital admission was public transportation. She was crying as she boarded the bus, and the other passengers grew silent. They understood something horrible had happened to this woman.

Polio and its resulting chain of events shaped my life. I was not quite three and forced to grow up quickly. With few opportunities to express my reaction to the emotional upheaval thrust upon me, I became a tough little cookie. Make no mistake, however, I was traumatized by polio, the subsequent treatment I received, and the disruption of my young life. The effects of the trauma lingered for many years.

After an initial period of hospitalization, the common treatment for polio in the 1950s was to place children in residential rehabilitation centers to receive the physical therapy needed to return to independence. In striking contrast, I had only been toilet trained for a few months and still could not dress myself without assistance. Nevertheless, I found myself living with a bunch of strangers in an institution called The Industrial Home for Crippled Children (The Home).

The Home was a large, red-brick structure situated in a residential neighborhood in Pittsburgh called Squirrel Hill. It resembled the other homes, real homes, in its neighborhood. Visiting hours at The Home were Saturdays and Sundays from two to four p.m., and for the next fourteen months, I only saw my parents four hours each week.

The primary responsibility at The Home for this influx of children who had polio was to assess the extent of damage to muscles and provide physical therapy to restore function. In my case, the main damage was to my right leg, which never regained any function; thus it became known as my "bad leg" or "floppy leg." There was also considerable muscle weakness in my left leg (the good leg), my back, abdomen, and neck. My arms were spared and were strengthened further through physical therapy to compensate for the muscle losses elsewhere in my body.

Although I have that one vivid memory of being in the hospital cubicle while two nurses laid heavy sandbags across my legs, I recall very little of my new life at The Home. Living away from my parents for fourteen months at such a young age, however, caused me to experience occasional panic attacks throughout childhood and ongoing feelings of emptiness and inadequacy. I also have had difficulty in building meaningful connections with others, presumably due to my fear of loss.

Hard Knock Life

Physical therapy is an unnatural experience for a three-year-old. Back when I was a little kid, my physical therapy (PT) following polio took place at The Home for Crippled Children. I served two sentences there, one beginning on or about my third birthday that lasted fourteen months and the second at the age of eleven for a period of seven months. I hated the name of this place, though kept it to myself, grateful I suppose that they dropped the word *Industrial* from its name at least. Think about it—what would you expect to see if you sent your child to The Industrial Home for Crippled Children—possibly Tiny Tim breaking rocks on a chain gang?

Perhaps my experience at The Home is the reason I love the play *Annie* so much. How many people can relate to a group of cute little girls singing, "It's a Hard Knock Life"? I certainly can. While I was not forced to scrub floors, I was confronted daily by the physical therapy grind. What else was there to do, after all? I was too young for school, so they had to concoct some sort of activity schedule to warrant keeping me there for over a year. Let's face it; there was only so much brace-fitting and doctor-visiting to be done.

By age four, I had had enough and, like Annie, sought an escape. I asserted myself one morning before Orthopedic Clinic, a monthly ordeal with a cast of a thousand onlookers. Since I did not have a faithful canine companion named Sandy for protection, the thought of leaving the confines of The Home never occurred to me. Instead, I hid in a storage room. To this day, I am able to relive the rush of fear and excitement when I recall listening to the voices of the nurses, aides, and therapists scurrying past the storage room door as they conducted the Big Search for me. My first awareness of personal power came that day, even though they found me on time to visit the doc. I had made a statement about having my fill of the whole rehabilitation experience, and they all seemed to respect me for it. There were no repercussions, only an increased gentleness. The staff at The Home were a kindly group, not a Miss Hannigan among them.

I do not mean to imply that all the time spent in physical therapy was wasted. To the contrary, I learned many useful skills in PT, such as picking up pencils with my toes. I once mentioned this talent to a guy on a date who very reasonably asked, "Is there much call for that?" You just know when a fellow invalidates one of your greatest accomplishments that the relationship is doomed, and it was.

Another vivid memory of PT is of lifting weights, big ones. At age four, I was lifting ten-pound barbells. Pictures of me back then reveal I was well on the way to becoming the pediatric version of The Rock.

Then there were the muscle tests. You could say I learned failure at an early age, good preparation for future math tests, I suppose. Every so often the physical therapist would give me a standard muscle test, wherein I had to push, pull, and squeeze so that she could determine which muscles worked and to what degree. To be honest, I don't think there was ever much change in my polio-ravaged muscles. Much like the 1960s-era comedic duo of Bob Williams and his underperforming dog Louie, who ignored the commands to "jump, boy, jump" or "roll over, boy," most of my muscles would remain immobile no matter how much they were coaxed, cajoled, and promised Olympic medals.

Overcompensating was the single greatest lesson instilled in me by those countless hours of PT, though. Just as my working muscles were taught to pull more than their share of the load, it was only a matter of time until I learned to push myself to the limit in all facets of life by becoming an overachiever with an exaggerated sense of responsibility.

GREAT FALLS I'VE TAKEN

Cathy Owen

By Betty F. Lennon

Winter returned last Friday morning with a vengeance. Folks everywhere were complaining how long winter was lasting—how difficult it was to get around—how trying it was to cope with winter's dirt—how this and that disrupted our daily routine. As I walked into the Industrial Home for Crippled Children on Denniston avenue, about noon that day, I suddenly realized that, in most cases, we create and build-up our own troubles, and can't see our neighbors who are faced with problems rightfully causing heartache. I was there to visit the two little girls pictured here, who are convalescing from Polio at the Home. These are Wilkinsburg children, who are receiving tender, almost "mother-like" care from the competent staff who run the Home.

Here you find 72 youngsters who must face life, handicapped. Yet, never have I seen a happier group of little folks. Many are victims of polio, yet others have been crippled since birth.

The house children, those who can get around without too much help, were on their way to lunch. A happy group of the youngsters were proud of their gold stars on their foreheads, they had been especially good that morning in kindergarten. Children who are able, attend classes, but those who are in the infirmary have bedside tutors.

Going upstairs to where Cathy and Darlene are still confined I found these little girls being dressed for the "picture taking". Nothing seemed too much trouble for the nurses who dressed the children with utmost care

Darlene Carnahan

Parents are allowed to visit for an hour every Saturday and Sunday.

Once a month these parents meet. They are known as the Parent's Organization and try in every way to assist the Home. This week Mr. and Mrs. A. H. Carnahan of Taylor way, and Mr. and Mrs. Gwilym Owen of Woodlawn avenue, parents of Cathy and Darlene, told me that the group is planning a benefit, the proceeds of which will be used for a drug fund there at the home. Wilkinsburgers who are interested in such a worthwhile project can learn further details by calling Mr. Carnahan at Fr 1-4181, or the Owens at Fr 1-3251.

These folks hope you have

(Continued on Page 12)

TRY THIS

The great Montgomery Ward Company got the biggest seventy-five cent shock of their existence last week when they placed a small help wanted advertisement in the Gazette and got forty-six clients by Monday evening and employment is the highest in the Nation's history.

A lady on Wright street advertised a small apartment. The Gazette appeared on the newstands about 9 o'clock and calls started. For the next three days the lady listened to the constant ring of the telephones. She got a desirable tenant.

A Gazette seventy-five-cent classified advertisement is the best investment for profits since the nickel cone was invented.

News article from The Wilkinsburg Gazette, February 1, 1951

2

Surviving Alone

Suffice it to say, I regressed developmentally during my initial hospitalization period of approximately one month following the diagnosis of polio. The aforementioned toilet training had disappeared by the time I arrived at The Home, and my mother was reprimanded for not having her four-year-old potty-trained. Four-year-old? Wow. I was barely three, though tall for my age. This disturbing assumption created unrealistic expectations and launched me into a lifetime of pretending to be older, wiser, and more confident than I was. Attempting to meet others' expectations during my formative years added stress to my already traumatized self.

The Home has had some truly remarkable staff throughout its history. Its name has changed several times over the years, but it has continually offered outstanding services to both children and adults with various disabilities. For me, the two most memorable staff were Virginia Whitfield, physical therapist, and Belle Grierson, social worker. They remained involved with me for many years and both attended my wedding.

Ms. Whitfield was a taskmaster who barely concealed her disdain for whiny little girls, thus altering any inclination I had in that direction. She had high expectations for me, and I wanted her approval. Ms. Grierson was the family liaison who frequently underscored the need for families to treat their children who had experienced polio normally. When we fell, our parents were told not to help us back to our feet, but to allow us to get up on our own. Ms. Whitfield's job was to make sure we walked again and were able to get back up after falling.

I lived at The Home for fourteen months until two months after my fourth birthday. My parents were often joined by my aunts during those cherished weekend visiting hours. Toward the end of my time at The Home, I was able to go to my real home for weekends. By then, I wore a brace on my right leg, extending from my foot and ending with a pelvic band around my hips. My right shoe had been modified with steel bands to accommodate where my brace was inserted. Because of the cost of orthopedic shoes, I only ever had one pair at a time. My choices were ugly shoes or even uglier ones. At that time, I used wooden under-arm crutches to walk. Ms. Whitfield had made sure

I was able to walk, run, go up and down steps without holding onto the railing, and knew how to fall. Yes, that's right, she taught me to fall so that I did not get tangled in my crutches and would not sustain injuries. The trick, of course, was to let go of or possibly throw aside my crutches. Ms. Whitfield's coaching on how to do stairs may have been her greatest accomplishment, given that I navigated a million or more steps without ever tumbling down them.

My relationship with The Home did not end when I was discharged. I was seen at the outpatient clinic by my orthopedist and his team until I graduated from high school. My "brace work" was also done there, including new braces as I grew and repairs when they would break, which was often. Being treated normally meant that I wore those "steel wonders" hard. Playgrounds, hopscotch, sled riding, kickball, I did it all!

I wonder why psychologists did not warn about how emotionally damaging it was for young children to be separated from their parents for even short periods. Apparently, they did not, or else no one listened. Was it necessary for a rehabilitation center to be a residential program? Honestly, how much physical therapy could a child receive in a day? Two or three hours, including time in the therapy tank and/or pool, was the maximum on weekdays. Weekends were therapy-free. Wouldn't money have been better spent on daily transportation so children could remain at home with loving families? It took many years for me to emotionally recover from the trauma of polio and separation from my parents.

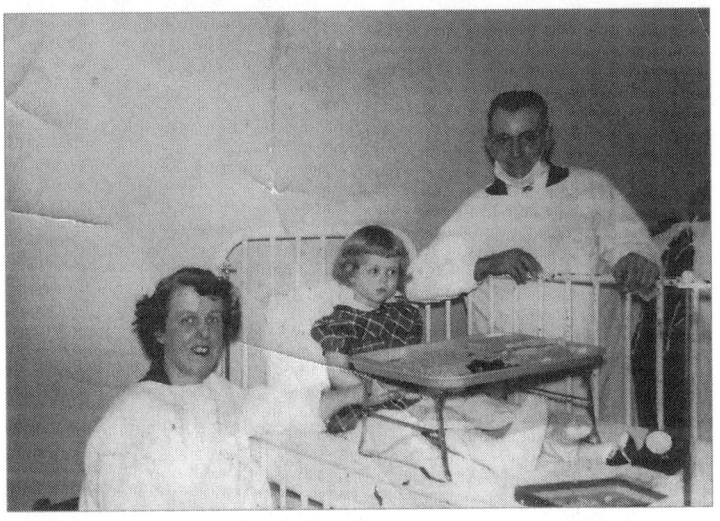

I had been at The Home for Crippled Children in Pittsburgh, Pennsylvania about two months when this photo and the one on the next page were taken of me with my parents.

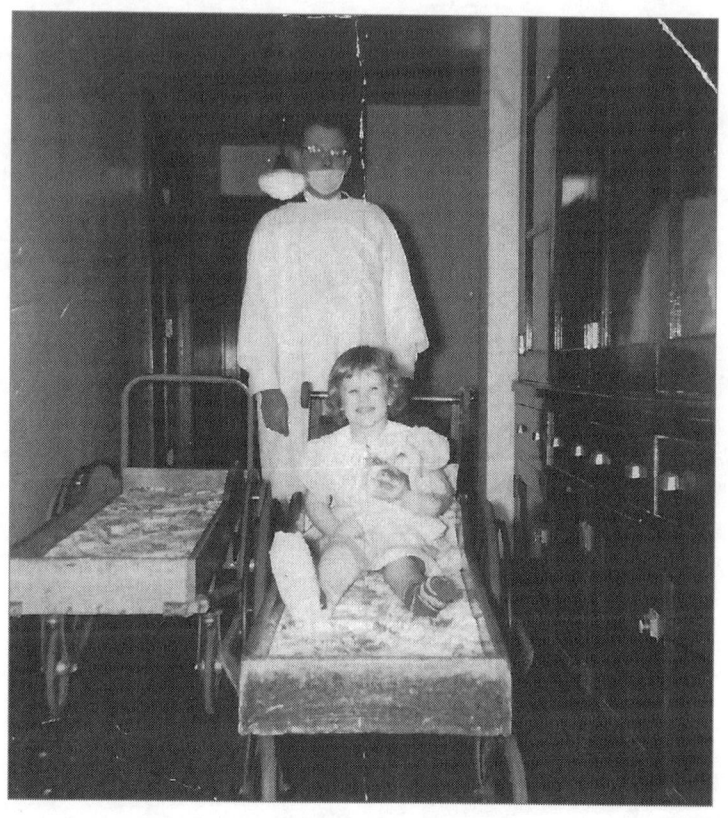

Here I am with my dad. I was three years old.

3

Strong Families Build Resilient Kids

I was an only child born to parents who had married relatively late. My father, Gwilym, emigrated from Wales with his family when he was eight years old. Being the oldest of seven children, he had to quit school after the sixth grade to help support the family. Initially, he worked in the coal mines in Northeastern Pennsylvania but switched to truck driving when he was old enough to obtain his license. After marrying my mother, he wanted to be at home every night with his family. He began hauling steel pipes for a local trucking company, earning far less than if he had continued long-distance, big-rig trucking. My dad and I were good friends, and I never doubted that he adored me.

My mother, Dorothy, was a homemaker until I was in junior high school, when she returned to the workforce to increase our family's meager income. She worked in the receiving room at a local department store tagging incoming products before they were sent to the floor for sale.

As a three-person family, we were a close-knit group, made even closer by living in a tiny, four-room bungalow. My mother and I had a loving, yet often contentious relationship due in large part to my living away from her for the fourteen months after having polio. She once told me that upon returning from The Home, I no longer needed her. Although I was more functionally independent than most four-year-old children, I also was emotionally damaged from my early childhood experiences and needed my mom to adapt to our rather unique situation.

Certainly, I wanted to live at home with my parents, but I had already been apart from and survived without them for a lengthy period. While other children my age had fears of being away from their mommies, I had endured a lengthy separation and become strong and independent. When I returned home at age four, not only could I tie my own shoes, but I could encase myself in my brace with its multiple laces and buckles. I had learned a new routine at The Home, and my mother suddenly found herself dealing with a teenage attitude wrapped in a little kid's body. Whereas other parents are introduced to adolescence gradually, mine were confronted by it with little warning or a chance to prepare.

The combination of my independence and the lingering effects of my early childhood trauma was the source of friction between my mother and me. Our difficult interactions were exacerbated by my mother's sometimes inflexible reactions to situations that required understanding and patience. One instance that stands out in my memory involved my thumb-sucking. Without the comfort of my doll, Janie, who had been seized and burned at the hospital due to having polio germs, I had turned to my left thumb for comfort. I depended on it, but only at night. My mother decided when I was five that thumb-sucking was a habit to be broken lest it damage my permanent teeth. At bedtime, she painted my thumb with a pungent liquid she had purchased at the drugstore. During the night, though, my left thumb would still find its way into my mouth. Since I lived to tell this story, I assume this foul-tasting product was not poison. I outlasted her attempts to distance me from my thumb and sucked it at night until sometime in high school. Interestingly, I had the insight to tell her more than once that I would give up thumb-sucking when I no longer needed it. Mom was right, though; all that thumb-sucking moved my pearly whites until they were quite crooked.

Throughout my elementary school years, when we disagreed or I misbehaved, my mother would threaten to send me to reform school. She clearly did not recognize the trauma I had sustained by my hospitalization and subsequent placement at The Home when I was so young, and it may have been the worst thing she could have said to me. My interpretation undoubtedly was, "If you sent me away once, you wouldn't hesitate to do it again."

My aunts were my salvation. My mother had a bunch of unmarried sisters who all lived together in a neighboring town. Aunt Katherine, in particular, was the buffer between my mother and me. With her abundance of love and patience, Aunt Katherine always made me feel valued and cherished during phone calls and visits. She possessed a natural caregiving ability and worked as a nurse's aide at her community hospital. When I was in elementary school, she left the workforce to care for their older sister who was recovering from a stroke. Each summer beginning in junior high, I would spend at least two weeks at the big house with Aunt Katherine, respite that I very much needed and appreciated. Canning peaches or rhubarb, preparing homemade applesauce and tending to her small backyard garden kept me busy. She taught me to embroider, and it was a pastime I relished during difficult times in my life.

I looked forward to the arrival of two other aunts, Margaret and Rachel, each weekday after work. Aunt Margaret would spend time in the evenings teaching me to knit. My philanthropic aspirations and actions can be traced to my Aunt Margaret, one of the most generous people I have ever known. Aunt Rachel and her young adult daughter Carol lived on the third floor of the big house along with Aunt Margaret. The third floor was a magical place with Aunt Margaret's collection of yarns and fabric scraps, Aunt Rachel's jewelry, and Carol's makeup. Carol willingly allowed me to practice applying her makeup, and I delved into it whenever I visited.

My father also had two sisters. Although I was not quite as close to those aunts, one of them, Aunt Blodwen, clearly understood the tension between my mother and me, and often jokingly reminded me that I could live with her if I ever grew tired of my parents. His other sister, Aunt Nelly, was quiet and kind. Her younger daughter, Sandy, became one of my best friends.

While we spent considerable time with my mother's family and somewhat less with my dad's, his was the fun family and quite prolific. I had many paternal cousins and second cousins, and it seemed there was always something to celebrate. Parties and picnics were a regular occurrence, and their wedding receptions were lively with lots of polka dancing. This cultural blending occurred because my dad's youngest brother, Uncle Glyn, had married into a Polish family. The food at these family gatherings was scrumptious, and I especially loved the halupki and kielbasa.

My aunts' kindnesses, enormous support, and close friendship were a constant as I grew up. They are gone now, and while I do not recall many specifics of my interactions with them, I regularly reflect with gratitude upon their warmth and their combined influence in my life.

Although my relationship with my mother was not ideal, I loved her and respected her. She heeded the recommendations of the professionals at The Home and engaged with them as needed. Their overarching philosophy was that parents should treat their children with polio as they would any other child. Thanks to this advice and their good instincts, my parents had the same expectations for me as every other parent in our community had for their children. They raised me to believe my life would have the same trajectory as that of my peers, and all other family members followed their lead by communicating similar messages. I recall my mother telling me more than once that I could realize whatever goals I set for myself – "just look at President Roosevelt," also a polio survivor who had led our country through the Great Depression and World War II. Ironically, my mother also repeatedly told me that I was not "crippled" even though I spent a good deal of time at The Home for Crippled Children.

My mother was a dedicated volunteer fund raiser for the March of Dimes.

4

In Search of...Role Models

Who am I? What will I become? Will anyone ever love me? Will I get married? Will I have children? Perhaps I had a greater sensitivity to my circumstances than most children, but I was searching for role models from a young age.

Growing up in the 1950s had its advantages. Life was simple. Going to school, playing with my neighborhood friends, and reading were my main adventures. Finding an adult role model with a visible disability, however, was like discovering an oasis in the middle of the desert.

My biological grandparents were deceased by the time I was born. I observed other children interacting with their grandparents and envied them. When I was seven, my parents and I visited the church attended by my aunts and uncles. I noticed an elderly woman enter from a side door near the altar. She was being pushed in her wheelchair by her husband. They sat in the second row, visible from my seat midway back. I watched them throughout the church service wondering why she used a wheelchair and whether she had grandchildren. How would she feel if I approached her when the church service ended? I imagined as a church-going person, she would have a kind heart. Afterwards, while my family conversed with friends, I wandered off, edging closer to the woman and her husband until I was in the woman's line of vision. She smiled and motioned me forward.

These were the Fosters, and they became my adopted grandparents. Grandma Foster was an amputee and Grandpa Foster was devoted to her. They had one biological granddaughter who was now a young adult and lived in the Midwest. They rarely saw her. Thus, our informal adoption of each other was mutually beneficial. Our relationship began when they invited my parents and me to visit them at their home, and what a home it was! Grandma Foster had a modest, one-person elevator that she used to travel between the first and second floors of their home. I never tired of riding in it during our visits. She also had a porch lift that she used to go from their back porch to the lower patio. Their car was in the garage behind the lower patio, and riding the porch lift was how Grandma entered and left their home.

My relationship with the Fosters continued through my college years but ended shortly after when Grandma passed away. Interactions with my adopted grandparents opened my eyes to the possibilities for people with disabilities through assistive technology. Equally valuable was seeing Grandpa Foster's devotion to his wife with a disability. It was reassuring to me, as I navigated my difficult teen years when I desperately wanted boyfriends but was shunned by most boys my age. Knowing there was a man who adored his wife, a wheelchair user, meant that there undoubtedly were other good men and that I might meet one someday.

The value of a close family role model with a disability cannot be overstated, but Grandma Foster had acquired her disability later in life and was elderly when I met her. As a young girl, I needed to know career possibilities and what the passage to adulthood might hold for someone like me. My well-meaning father wanted me to obtain secretarial skills so that I would not end up in a sheltered workshop. A worthy ambition, certainly, but I wanted more.

And then, magically, it happened, and where else than at The Home? I was thirteen or so and there for an orthopedic clinic visit. By this time, they were holding clinic in the basement brace shop. Si, the lead brace builder and fitter, whose professional title was upgraded much later to orthotist, was also a polio survivor. I never perceived him as a role model, though. His was a blue-collar profession, and I had no interest in it. His job required much standing, and I knew I would require a seated occupation.

As my mother and I walked across the lobby on our way to the elevator leading to the brace shop, I suddenly noticed a man pushing his wheelchair about fifty feet to my right. I jerked my head to look, but he was gone in a flash. What registered was that he was African American, and he was wearing a white shirt with a tie. Eureka! Here was someone employed at The Home in a professional capacity who experienced a disability. So rare was the view of an adult with a disability in the 1960s that catching a glimpse of this man became a highlight of my quarterly clinic visits. Being a shy girl, I never asked to meet him but did learn his name and that he worked in the accounting department. The fact that I distinctly remember him nearly sixty years later speaks volumes about the importance of role models for children and youth with disabilities.

5

Moving to the 'Burbs

We lived in Pittsburgh when I contracted polio but moved to the suburbs when I was in the middle of first grade. My mother's wisdom precipitated the move. My elementary school in Pittsburgh required navigating two steep hills and twice crossing streets with considerable traffic. In fact, one of my classmates was struck by a vehicle while crossing one of the busy streets. Having my mother escort me to and from school in kindergarten and first grade was acceptable, but she understood my need for independence and knew that arrangement could not continue.

Although they could barely afford the new house in the suburbs, my parents chose to move, and I always understood it was a sacrifice for them. Most telling was that our house was the smallest and most sparsely landscaped in the neighborhood. It was a four-room bungalow with one bathroom. There were no front or back porches, and the basement was unfinished. Nor could my parents ever afford to upgrade this house. The large yard, however, suited my childhood needs for a small swing set.

The neighborhood compensated for the shortcomings of the house itself. There were fewer than forty houses on two dead-end streets running perpendicular to each other, and each had a large cul-de-sac. Our house backed to the woods. Beyond the woods was a farm, and when the cows began wandering into our yards, the farmer hastily added a barbed-wire fence.

Hopscotch, bike riding, kickball, sled riding, and a host of other activities were all safely executed in the two streets thanks to the limited traffic in the neighborhood. With many children of various ages, there was no shortage of friends and social interaction. We created and performed plays and held marathon games of Monopoly in the summer. My yard was a badminton center while others had more elaborate swing sets than the one in my yard.

To earn money for my badminton set, I sold greeting cards. This enterprising idea came from an advertisement in a kids' magazine to which my Aunt Margaret had subscribed for me. Greeting cards launched my career in sales. I did it again and again. Once I even made sit-upons from old newspapers and went door-to-door selling them. Clearly, I was a child with chutzpah. Who could resist buying something, even something worthless like a woven sit-upon painted metallic silver, from a cute little girl with braces and crutches? At a young age, I was learning the secret of telethon success.

The elementary school for my new neighborhood was multi-storied with no elevator. After I spent just a few days there, my neighborhood was re-districted to a single level school much farther away. The purpose of this was lost on me since the cafeteria at the new school was in the basement, and I had to do the steps once a day anyhow. Nevertheless, my new suburban school system had implemented the concept of "reasonable accommodation" many years prior to the introduction of that term in Section 504 of the Rehabilitation Act.

The school bus picked us up at the end of the street, which was about a two-block walk for me. This was not a problem, until the first snowstorm. Rarely was school ever canceled due to snow back then. Two neighbor boys, Rusty and Harry, took turns pulling me on my sled to the bus stop. We left the sled there until after school, and then they would haul me back home. This became a standard practice that continued throughout elementary school.

I met my best friend, Nancy Williamson, on the first day at my new school. Many years later she told me that our teacher had asked her to look out for me. Nancy had polio, too, but at a slightly older age than I did. Although she wore one leg brace, her other leg was strong, and she did not need crutches. We were together through fourth grade, and then her neighborhood was redistricted to a newly constructed school. Nancy and I remained "besties" through college and served as each other's maid and matron of honor at our respective weddings. After drifting apart for many years, we were reunited at our fiftieth high school reunion.

My first "great fall" occurred on the school playground when I was in second grade. I was playing kickball and fell while sauntering over to first base. Plunk. My chin hit the pavement first and required seven stitches to close the wound. I was back in school the next day, and unfortunately, it was school picture day.

6

My Defining Year

Early in the summer when I was ten years old, I had my first orthopedic surgery. My friend Nancy and another polio-surviving friend whose family attended my church were already experienced with orthopedic surgeries. My doctor, however, believed in waiting until muscles and bones were nearly finished growing. Even though I was older than my peers for my first surgery and had the benefit of hearing their experiences, I was truly terrified. I was convinced I was going to die. Undoubtedly, my intense fear was a remnant of my early childhood hospital experience when diagnosed with polio. It was PTSD before that concept and term became well-known.

A traffic issue impeded my parents' arrival at the hospital the morning of the surgery. By the time I saw them, I was in the throes of a full-blown panic attack. Nothing my parents or any nurse said could calm me. In the operating room, the anesthesiologist tried to inject me with sodium pentothal, but he could not find a vein as they had apparently shrunk from my fear. Instead, they sedated me with ether, and, of course, as I began to awaken, I was very nauseous, thus confirming my fears that surgery would be an awful experience. But, at least I survived.

Prior to the surgery, I wore a full leg brace on my right leg with a back brace attached and a half brace on my left to corral my left foot, which was hellbent on turning out at a forty-five-degree angle. The surgery was to correct the left leg issue and eliminate the need for the short brace on that leg. I used a wheelchair throughout the summer since no weight-bearing was permitted. No one told me to wear the right leg brace, so I enjoyed the freedom of being without it. Bad move.

Once the cast on my left leg was removed for the final time in late August, the plan was for me to stay overnight at The Home, be checked by my orthopedist, and then measured for a new right leg brace by the brace shop. However, my once-night stay turned into seven months. Not only were there infected sores on my left leg from being in a cast all summer, but the main bone in my right leg, the tibia, was now crooked from being unstructured by my brace for over two months. After a month of treatment for the infections and an attempt to straighten the right leg mechanically with splints and other devices, I was given the grim news—more surgery.

This time the cast extended from my foot to my hip, and I needed a wheelchair with a leg lift. This precluded my going home since I could not navigate my family's tiny bungalow with my leg extended. Following surgery, I had to recuperate and rehabilitate at The Home.

My understanding of my early childhood experiences at The Home would be nonexistent if I had not spent another seven months there when I was eleven years old. My memories of this time are vivid and all mine, not gleaned from conversations with my parents. They also give me a context for some of my adult feelings and choices.

The year was 1958, and I had a life-molding experience. The Home used a Red Cross volunteer called a "gray lady" to escort me and another girl to the hospital located on the other side of Pittsburgh. One could assume the term "gray lady" was used due to the color of her uniform, although she did have gray hair, which made me wonder.

The other girl had cerebral palsy and was not able to speak. She resided in the infirmary section of The Home, where she received personal care assistance. Those of us who could tend to our personal care lived in a section called "the house;" thus, I had never met this girl. It strikes me that sending two children to the hospital with a stranger was not a good idea. Sending a girl who could not verbally communicate with two people who she had never seen prior was insensitive at best. Even then, I must have understood the seriousness of her situation. I tried hard to understand her attempts at communicating and, possibly it was lucky guessing on my part or divine intervention, but I was able to understand and correctly convey what she was trying to say. The nurses on duty when we arrived placed us in adjoining beds, and I became her interpreter. I went for surgery as scheduled, but due to an upper respiratory infection, the girl's surgery was delayed.

I awakened to horrible pain and the need for heavy sedation over the course of the next four days. They had cut my tibia in half and reset the bone to straighten the leg, leaving raw nerve endings that caused the pain. I could no longer be the girl's interpreter, so my mother and Aunt Katherine took over. This girl's parents lived far away and were unable to make the trip to be with her. What my mom and aunt lacked in understanding her communication, they more than made up for by smothering her with kindness and attention. Ultimately, the girl's surgery was postponed indefinitely, and she went back to The Home. I never saw her again.

In reflecting on the hospital incident with the girl who was nonverbal, I now realize I became an advocate for other people with disabilities because of this experience at age eleven. This incident had a connection to my choice of college major, i.e., speech and hearing disorders, as did my friendship with an older girl who was rehabilitating at The Home following surgery. This older girl named Lynn was in her first year of high school, whereas I had yet to finish elementary school. In spite of our age difference, we had much in common. We stayed in touch for several years, and I wanted to do everything Lynn did. She went to Bowling Green University and majored in speech pathology, so I applied to the same college for the same major. Unfortunately, the vocational rehabilitation agency in my state would not pay out-of-state tuition, and, since my parents were relatively poor, it was imperative that I attend a Pennsylvania college.

This unexpected seven-month residential placement at The Home was a huge disappointment for me. I wanted to be in sixth grade at Jordan Elementary School with my friends. I missed them, my family, and my neighborhood. I was institutionalized, though as institutions go, it was a comfortable one with kind and friendly staff. One saving grace was my love of reading. The Home had a small and seldom-used library. I wandered in there shortly after my arrival and discovered a trove of Nancy Drew books, including the older, original ones I had not read. I immersed myself in them over the next few weeks. By the time I finished with Nancy Drew, I had made new friends and was settled into a daily routine.

I lived in the section of The Home called the "house" in which there were four wards, two for girls and two for boys. I was placed in the "big girls ward." The little girls' ward ended at age ten and the big girls' ward began at age twelve. Being eleven years old put me at an in-between age and meant I was the youngest resident of the "big girls" ward. There were twelve beds in my ward, six on each side of a large room. At one end of the room there were dressers, and we each had a drawer for our belongings. At the other end of the room were closets, and we each had a section of the closet. We big girls shared a single bathroom that had two toilets separated by a curtain, two sinks, and one tub. Privacy did not exist. The big girls' ward had a lounge with a TV and tables for games and crafts. Monday nights were craft nights. A woman, possibly a recreational therapist, would bring art supplies, paint-by-number kits and snacks. We would crowd into our lounge and do activities with her.

My sex education occurred at The Home. A year earlier, when I was about ten years old, my mother gave me a little booklet entitled *Growing Up and Liking It* to prepare me for the surprises yet to come.

I was so stunned to learn about menstruation that I did not absorb much else in the book. When the lights went out at The Home, the conversation about love and sex began in the "big girls" ward. Not wanting to embarrass myself through a show of ignorance, I mostly listened and frequently pretended to know more than I actually did. By and large, the information was accurate, and I seemed to be just the right age and in the right circumstances to absorb it.

The sex education was timely for two reasons. First, my friend Lynn had a boyfriend who let her know that another boy was interested in me. His name was Joe, and he was a year older than me. Joe had a minimal physical disability that caused him to limp. The four of us would get together twice a week in the evenings in a seating area outside the staff office located between the boys' wards and the girls' wards. Lynn and her boyfriend kissed, so Joe and I occasionally followed suit. Joe and I exchanged letters for a few years after I went home, and I returned to visit him once before he was discharged.

The second reason the sex education was timely was more nefarious. There was an evening shift attendant on the older boys' ward who should not have been working around minors. I almost had a "#metoo experience." While they were attempting to straighten my leg using splints, I was moved around on a gurney while lying in a prone position. Vulnerable, extremely vulnerable. This predator would make sure to push my gurney every Friday evening to the recreation room on the first floor, where there was a movie, games, or live entertainment. He always made sure we were alone in the elevator. Fortunately, kissing was as far as he progressed, and it ended once I had surgery. I often wondered if he had moved on to one of the other girls while I was hospitalized. When I was back at my own home, I mentioned this casually, but intentionally, during a conversation with my mother. I returned once to visit friends at The Home and learned the man no longer worked there. My mother had swiftly, but quietly, reported the predator, as I knew she would.

Food became a big deal in my life at The Home. The head of the dietary department was a registered dietician, a dour woman somewhat beyond middle age. She made no attempt at creative, child-friendly cuisine. There was never a smiley face on our pancakes, and Friday nights featured the repetitious meal from hell—fish of some sort, bland mac-and-cheese, and stewed tomatoes. I refused to eat it and went to bed hungry every Friday night. Fortunately, the next day was a visiting day, and my Aunt Katherine always either brought or sent something homemade and delicious. I believe my problematic relationship with food and resulting weight problems that have lasted throughout my adult life began at The Home. If I found Friday night dinners revolting at age eleven, I can only imagine how little I ate as a three-year-old.

The Home offered a school for its residents, so I began sixth grade there. The other kids in my class varied in age from eleven to eighteen. I learned how fortunate I was to have a minor disability that resulted in my being welcome at my neighborhood school. Most of my classmates at The Home had more significant disabilities and had not been included in public school classrooms. They had experienced hit-or-miss homebound instruction or had attended less-than-challenging classes organized by parents. As a result, they were years behind and struggling to do sixth grade work.

My transition back to my home school after seven months at The Home can best be described as uncomfortable. Whereas I was an outstanding student at The Home, I was lagging behind when I returned to my home school. The Russians had sent Sputnik up the year before, and my school district quickly introduced science in grades four to six. On my first day back, the lesson was on photosynthesis, and I was completely lost, for there had been no science instruction at The Home.

As much as I wanted to return to my home and public school, I was fearful and had become dependent on the security of The Home. This phenomenon happened to me again as an adult when I was uneasy about leaving the hospital following surgery for an ectopic pregnancy. What I experienced both times was not exactly "learned helplessness," which is when a person believes they cannot change their situation, but it was a close relative called "learned dependency."

The Splinter

Having a splinter embedded under your thumbnail is not a big deal unless, of course, you happen to be a kid with a disability. Then, even a small mishap can become a medical event of gargantuan proportions. And so it happened when I was eleven years old and, thanks to an emerging adolescent cynicism, I was able to appreciate a truly ridiculous situation.

It happened about two weeks before I was to leave The Home for Crippled Children, where I was trying desperately not to become socially and emotionally crippled as a result of a one-day admission that had dragged on for seven months. I had done my time in a Hubbard tank, a splint, a cast, and a wheelchair that looked like it had been used by our thirty-second president or come straight from the set of *Sunrise at Campobello*. Now I was ready to leave.

To prepare me for the transition from the pseudo fix-it world of rehab to the real world, was none other than my school nurse, Mrs. Monica Schuckers, a comforting presence. Mrs. Schuckers was my friend and had been my supporter throughout elementary school. Sending her to The Home was the school's way of acknowledging that my transition back to my home school might not be as easy as I assumed. How right they were!

Seeing Mrs. Schuckers caused my natural exuberance to surface. I was simultaneously smiling, talking, and gesturing emphatically. I paid scant attention to the decrepit table before me in the antiquated classroom as I talked with Mrs. Schuckers, and that was how the nasty old splinter found its way under my thumbnail.

After Mrs. Schuckers left, I was sent to the infirmary where they clipped, tweezed, and swabbed but had no luck ousting the culprit. Plan B was to suck out the splinter using some sort of paint-on medication and then encasing the thumb in a plastic bag to create a vacuum. When Plan B alone failed, it was supplemented with Plan C. Plan C was my favorite because, in an attempt to soak out the splinter, I got to swim twice a day.

After a week of squeezing, tweezing, soaking, and painting, not to mention wearing the plastic bag that made my thumb look like an animator had drawn it for a Tom and Jerry cartoon, the splinter was still there.

The nurses from the infirmary next took the common-sense approach and did what any level-headed person would do to remove a splinter—they sent me to a hospital on the other side of the city to see my orthopedist! Nobody, however, bothered to tell this bone and muscle expert why he was seeing me. He walked in, barely said hello—I was thirty-five before I met a doctor with a personality—and told me to get undressed down to my underwear and he'd be right back.

Upon his return, I was asked to do my usual routine—

- walk toward him—OK
- walk away from him—Fine
- hop up on the table and take off my brace—WHOA!

Even when you're eleven years old and all alone in a hospital cubicle with a doctor who never smiles and barely talks, there is a limit to the nonsense you can endure. So I innocently asked, "Why do I need to take off my brace just to get this splinter out?"

"Splinter?"

"Yes, see..."

"Hmmm, no one told me about the splinter."

He may not have been much of a talker, but he cut that nail back quickly and painlessly and removed the splinter all within a few minutes, proving that sending me to an orthopedic surgeon was indeed a brilliant idea.

PART 2
ADOLESCENCE IS NOT FOR THE FAINT HEARTED

7

Fitting In Again

I returned to my family and community school from The Home in April and had a limited time to reintegrate myself before the school year ended. For those final two months of sixth grade, I felt like a speedskater trying to catch up to the pack both academically and socially. Summer vacation could not arrive too soon!

On the home front, my seven month separation from my parents did nothing to improve my relationship with my mother. I had become more confident in my decision-making ability without any maternal input. Exacerbating our situation was my growing adolescent attitude. There was friction at every turn!

In my school district, grades seven through nine were in junior high. Throughout, I felt secure academically, though I continued to lag behind in science. My extracurricular social activities revolved around my church youth group and Friday night dances at my school. These dances were well attended. The dancers and observers were inside the gym while the outer hallway was filled with those who preferred flirting, exchanging a little gossip, and/or genuine conversation. I stayed mostly inside as an observer, yearning to dance but too self-conscious to show my moves.

My close relationship with my father continued. As a reward for his unconditional love, I became a sports fan. He was passionate about baseball and football. During the short time in the fall when both sports were being played, he would watch one game on TV while listening to the other on his transistor radio propped between his neck and shoulder. His dual-game approach irritated my mother, who had no interest in sports. Due to the small size of our house and the fact that the poor woman did not drive, my mother was trapped between competing game announcers with hypernasality.

Baseball captured my attention first. I began attending Pittsburgh Pirate games in junior high with my church youth group. Tickets cost $1.50 (really!), and right field at the quaint Forbes Field was reserved on Saturdays for this "knothole" contingent of young people and chaperones. There we were afforded a closeup view of the late, great Roberto Clemente, the Pirates' right fielder. We cheered for him and, being annoying 'tweens, sometimes tried to get his attention by dropping our sunglasses, wallets, and other items on the field before the game started. Sweet man that he was, Roberto stoically retrieved them for us. Once the games began, there was always excitement in right field, for Roberto Clemente had a cannon of an arm and would cut down opposing team baserunners trying to stretch singles into doubles or score on fly balls. Seeing my interest in baseball, my father occasionally would get tickets through his company for Pirate games and take my best friend Nancy and me, where we were treated to an exceptional view in field-level box seats.

Many years later, I tacked football onto my list of sports interests when the Pittsburgh Steelers fielded their amazing teams in the 1970s. My dad and I would joyfully converse by phone when they won playoff games and four Super Bowls.

Coming to Grips with Reality

In the fall before my family moved to the suburbs, my dad and I walked up the hill on Friday nights to watch the high school band marching to the football field. By then I was six years old. I loved seeing the majorettes and aspired to become one someday. One of my aunts gave me a baton for my birthday, and I commenced practicing. As a child, my vision of my sixteen-year-old self was always as an able-bodied teen. Throughout elementary school, I was a majorette in training.

After celebrating my thirteenth birthday at a large family gathering, I was alone in my room. I sat quietly on my bed and acknowledged for the first time that I would still have a disability at age sixteen and most likely forever. I shed a few tears, then consoled myself by listening to records on my high-fidelity record player. Ahhh, music, the salvation of my soul.

It was time to develop new dreams for my future, a future that included accepting myself as a young woman with a disability. That night, I vowed to begin doing so.

Undies

As an alum of The Home for Crippled Children, I had to be seen at the outpatient orthopedic clinic two to four times a year. Being "seen" is meant in its most literal sense, with lots of spectators and dressed in only my underwear. All the easier to view those crooked body parts! In reflecting on my youth, it sometimes seems as if I spent half of it in my undies, which was all right between the ages of three and ten, but after that my sensitivities began to develop, not to mention other physical attributes.

Outpatient clinics at The Home were somewhat like fairy-tale stepchildren. Although everyone recognized the need to have them, they tended to be an added nuisance, disrupting the daily routine of the staff who had to attend them. Perhaps that was why the clinics were constantly moved, from the physical therapy department to the brace shop, to the stage. Really! The stage was probably my favorite place because it was bright and airy, unlike the dingy brace shop in the basement. The stage also appealed to my sense of adventure since I could never be sure if I'd be parading around in my underwear for just the docs and allied health professionals or whether custodians, cooks, and office staff might decide to take in the peep show. Unfortunately, those cute little spandex shorts and shirts had not been invented when I really needed them. And why didn't our clever mothers think to have us wear bathing suits, which would have been less revealing than bras and panties? But, I digress.

Clinic-on-Stage was fast-paced, not only because the docs had little time to waste, but also because the adjacent auditorium doubled as a lunchroom. Clinic had to be over before the meal began—probably some sort of Health Department rule not to mix food serving with body checking.

The focus of these orthopedic clinics was on bodily flaws and the correction thereof. The better you looked, the less time the entourage spent with you. But, boy, if you had a spinal curvature, you could count on being gawked at while standing, walking, sitting, lying down, and balancing on one foot while you whistled the "Hallelujah Chorus."

Aside from my scoliosis, which my orthopedist thought did not warrant major surgery followed by a year in a body cast, my main flaw was a two-inch difference in the length of my legs. At every visit they would poke at my hip until they got my legs lined up, but the measurement was always the same—my right leg was two inches shorter than the left, no more, no less. Each time they seemed to be hoping for an additional one-eighth inch so they could justify "slicing," aka surgical intervention, to slow the growth of my better leg.

Having one leg that's two inches shorter than its mate is no big deal—you limp a little. They all missed the truly significant problem. My right foot was two shoe sizes smaller than my left. Now this was a bodily flaw with major financial and fashion implications. Try finding matching shoes in sizes 5½ and 3½. It's like having one foot stuck in childhood.

For years, I have wondered whether a job applicant can be taken seriously wearing a dressed-for-success navy blue suit and a pair of Mary Janes. Explain that to the EEOC staff investigating your hiring discrimination complaint and watch their eyes glaze over. More digression.

The entourage alluded to earlier was a formidable group of professionals and students who moved almost silently through the clinic, with only the rustling of starched uniforms to warn of their approach. The group included orthopedists, orthopedic residents, physical therapists and their interns, nurses, nursing students, a social worker, and two brace men who changed their titles to orthotists when I was about fourteen, finally sounding like they belonged in medi-land instead of with Amtrak. The size of the entourage was directly proportional to The Home's reputation. As it became the toast of the rehabilitation field, the entourage grew to more than twenty-five (although it seemed like 1,000), making any attempt at modesty a travesty.

The most important part of any orthopedic exam seemed to be walking, first away from the docs, then toward them. I was convinced I was in training for the Miss America Pageant. Due to cramped quarters, this strut, minus a serenade, had to occur outside the relative privacy of the cubicle. At that point, it became time for prayer that the adolescent boy patients would remember the "golden rule" and not peek from behind their curtains. Another source for embarrassment was the presence of residents, most of whom were attractive foreign-born men in their late twenties. There was no avoiding their penetrating gazes. They were still learning and always eager to hear the head doc reminisce about the partial triple arthrodesis he had performed on my left ankle. Apparently, a lousy bedside manner is not unique to the United States, since all but one of these junior docs who had come from South American countries were just as robotic as the "made in the USA" types. Perhaps they were afraid that the head doc would chew them up and spit them out if they said anything. I know I was.

Learning to speak up to the medical professionals was indeed a challenge. I believe my youthful attempts to be taken seriously while in my underwear were great practice for my adult role as a disability advocate having to negotiate with intransigent bureaucrats. It may be the basis for my willingness to take risks, too; after all, when you're down to your undies, you have little more to lose. Since "public stripping and strutting" is a phenomenon common to many of us with physical disabilities in my generation, it also may be one of the secret sources of power behind the disability rights movement in this country.

9

Teen Angst

The best that can be said about high school was that it only lasted three years, although it seemed like an eternity. Plagued by constant self-doubts and occasional self-loathing, I mostly wallowed in misery.

My plethora of insecurities could not be offset by having a core group of friends and some scattered fond memories. My lack of self-worth was reinforced by being ignored by the male species. I was in the passenger seat one evening when my girlfriend pulled her car into the new fast-food restaurant. The boys in the next car smiled flirtatiously and waved. Equally flirtatious, I returned their smiles. When I opened the door and began getting out, they all turned away in a quick, synchronized motion and did not look back. Ouch!

I believe my self-esteem was aligned with that of my peer group as I entered high school. I was attractive and dressed stylishly thanks to my Aunt Margaret and her credit card. I do not recall being self-conscious about my disability then. By the time I graduated, however, my self-esteem had plummeted. The self-acceptance I had enjoyed when I entered high school began to evaporate rapidly. As a teenager, it was difficult not to compare myself to my peers and be intimidated by my talented and high achieving classmates. Further, I was not invited to school dances and private parties where boys and girls paired off. Although high school was more than parties and dances, exclusion from these events distanced me from my peers. Suddenly, I had little to contribute to conversations at lunchtime and between classes.

There was no one with whom I felt comfortable talking about my feelings of dejection. I remember wanting some reassurance that the emotional roller coaster of adolescence would end, and my life would improve. I longed to know the experiences of disabled adults with college, jobs, marriage, and family. I needed to know the future held promises and opportunities for success in various realms.

My mother noticed something was amiss early in my junior year and spoke to Ms. Grierson at The Home, thereby securing me a couple of sessions with a psychologist. He was a great help. When I shared my disappointment about the complete lack of interest from my male peers, I recall him saying, "You look in the mirror and see an attractive person, yet you get rejection from others." This was an aptly stated summary of my feelings at the time.

Besides music, what got me through these difficult years was an early boyfriend and some good girlfriends. As I mentioned earlier, I had a "bestie," fellow polio survivor Nancy, beginning in first grade at my new suburban elementary school when our teacher assigned her to look out for me when I transferred to this school in the middle of the school year. Although our paths separated after fourth grade when a new elementary school opened near her home, we stayed in touch and were reunited in high school. We never talked about our disabilities. It was not necessary for we shared an unspoken bond. Instead, we were caught up in the usual chit-chat about school, boys, makeup, clothing, movies, and everything else that teen girls talk about.

My other girlfriends and I went to the same church. There we all participated in a youth fellowship group that had great advisors who planned interesting activities. Staying busy and connected certainly benefitted me. In the summers, we all went to Presbyterian church camps for one week.

The summer before starting high school, I met my early boyfriend, Trez, at a church camp located on Lake Erie. He was a "preacher's kid" who worked at the camp for the entire summer. My teen perspective of him was that he was "soooooo cute." He was also polite and kind. We stayed in touch for several months via letters, phone calls, and a visit. In reflecting on this relationship, I now believe it was a seminal event in my life. Although I was dateless through three years of high school, one boy had puppy loved me; thus, I believed there would be others.

In addition to arranging a few sessions with the psychologist, Ms. Grierson offered me a volunteer position for the summer when I was sixteen. For me, it was back to The Home. Twice each week I spent six hours volunteering on what was called the "baby boys" ward. This ward was in the infirmary section of The Home and housed boys between eighteen months and four years old. They were cute kids with cerebral palsy and spina bifida. I diapered and dressed them and helped one little boy to eat since he could not feed himself. After their naps, I played with them.

For most teens, learning to drive is a long-anticipated rite of passage. My dad was a professional trucker, however, and wary of teen drivers, particularly one behind the wheel of our family's only car. Suffice it to say, I did not run out the door on my sixteenth birthday to get my learner's permit. I was forced to wait another year and watch while my friends obtained their licenses.

Senior activities began in the spring of 1965, one of those being the senior prom. My high school "datelessness" included not "being invited" to my senior prom. Being invited was a cultural norm in 1965. Nice girls waited to be invited by boys. My "Queen of the Prom" essay documents my situation and my somewhat regrettable, though progressive feminist, action.

Not attending my senior prom was almost anti-climactic. I was nearing the high school finish line and looking forward to a fresh start in college. In reflecting on my experience and on recent stories about teens with disabilities being taken to their proms by kind-hearted classmates or family friends, I truly am thankful to have been spared a charity date. As the saying goes, "What doesn't kill you makes you stronger," and the pain of loneliness on prom night, and throughout high school, for that matter, led to my personal growth and greater self-awareness.

Missing my senior prom was not the final indignity suffered in high school, however. While proceeding through the smorgasbord line at the senior banquet, my heel found a green bean and suddenly I was on the floor with other scraps of dropped food. This unforgettable moment caused me to skip class reunions for the next fifty years!

This is me with my "bestie", Nancy Williamson Edmondson, circa 1965.

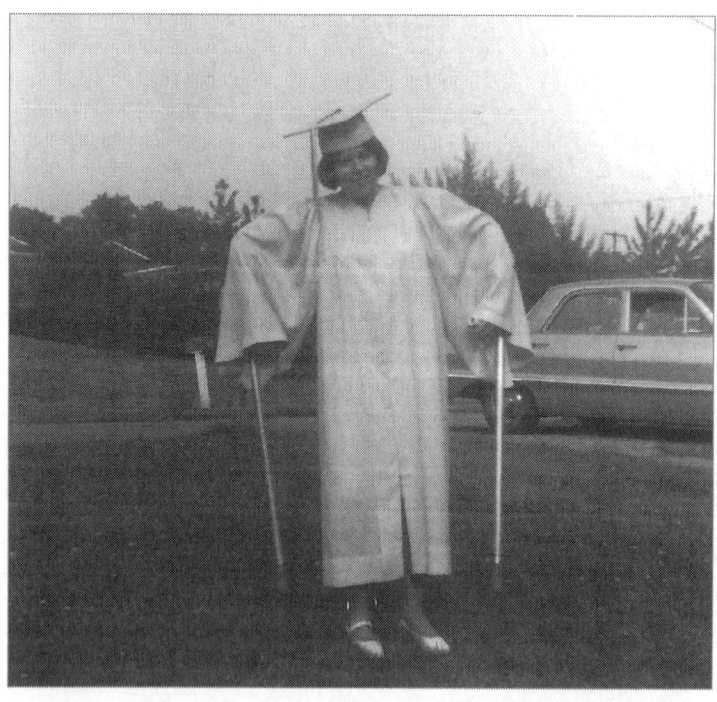

Was I happy to be graduating from high school? You betcha!

John Derrico, I Forgive You

He was the love of my life, or at least the object of my sophomoric fantasies. Not a guy you would describe as a hunk, necessarily; he was, nonetheless, starting fullback of the Gateway Gators and a junior!

Now, that being my first year of high school, I had yet to face any rejection. My family loved me, doted on me, and told me I was beautiful and witty. Being a self-absorbed teenager, I was convinced they were right, not biased. My friends included me, voted for me in school elections, and laughed at my jokes. How was I to realize I was too conspicuous?

But, I'm getting ahead of myself. Our relationship had progressed from a smile, to a "hi," to occasional chats at lunch or before classes started. I was convinced by that time I'd be a young bride.

The fatal end to this budding relationship happened as suddenly as it began to blossom. One day as I was walking to the gym, he fell in beside me. WOW!

The exhilaration was almost overwhelming. We laughed and talked. My heart was aflutter. Then, I felt it happen, and by that time there was no stopping it. His foot pushed firmly and swiftly against my crutch. CRASH! I was on the floor and after an eternity of stunned silence, people began helping me to rise again.

He was crimson-faced and oh so apologetic. I was equally red and ever so gracious. "No, no, I'm fine. I wasn't paying attention to where I was walking. Please don't feel bad." We smiled, but we both knew the relationship was over. He raced off to the gym to build more muscles, and I trotted to the ladies' room to regain my composure.

We coexisted for another year and a half, reverting to pleasant smiles and hellos. He dated other girls and I had mad crushes on other boys—but no dates, for I had violated the cardinal rule of teens everywhere, "Thou shall blend in."

We never really talked after that incident. For years, I've imagined him carrying around an enormous burden of guilt because he made a sweet young thing fall flat on her face. Finally, after all these years, I am ready to end his suffering. John Derrico, wherever you are, I FORGIVE YOU!

The Driving Lesson

My driving teacher was a "lech," as in lecherous middle-aged man with a pot belly. Actually, my father, who was not a lech, taught me to drive. However, Dad feared there was something mystical about teaching a person to drive who used hand controls instead of foot pedals. So, after countless white-knuckle rides with Dad trying to stop his left foot from making its involuntary braking motion, he decided I might benefit from a few lessons with a pro. It was too bad for Dad and his '63 Chevy Malibu that he didn't find a real pro.

The day of the first, and, what turned out to be the last, professional driving lesson dawned ominously. It was one of those autumn days that are barely distinguishable from autumn nights, complete with heavy rains and gusting winds that blow dead saturated leaves onto car windshields.

The thought of postponing the lesson due to inclement weather never crossed my freedom-obsessed mind. After all, I had turned seventeen and was mortified by my parents' decision not to let me get my license as soon as I turned sixteen like my friends. So intense was my goal of conforming with my peers, neither hell nor high water, even on the roads of suburban Pittsburgh, could deter me.

The professional driving teacher, hereafter referred to as the "pro," arrived in the driving school car complete with dual steering wheels. Since his car was not equipped with hand controls, however, we had to use my father's car which had hand controls installed. Off we went, heading for parts unknown. Literally. This guy took me to places I'd never been, all within thirty minutes of my house. That was okay with me, until I glanced over at him midway through this adventure and discovered he was sleeping. At least I hoped he was sleeping. I snuck a few more quick peeks at him to be sure he was still breathing and was relieved when he began to snore.

Not wishing to disturb Rip Van Winkle, I decided to turn back and retrace my path of travel. When I finally had returned to familiar territory, he awakened refreshed and with rejuvenated libido.

He placed his hand on my knee and began to tell me how attractive I was and not to be afraid of marrying an older man. Yikes! That I managed to avoid the road's soft shoulder as he massaged my muscular one was indeed a feat. I succeeded in making him retreat, wandering hands and all, to his side of the front seat by regaling him with a seemingly endless monologue about my college plans and my high school friends, teachers, and activities. Yes, this was the day I discovered a wondrous talent of controlling any guy who became a little too amorous by boring him to tears. Unfortunately, before I learned to use this gift sparingly, I may have scared off a few decent guys, as well.

At long last we were less than a mile and only one traffic light away from home. I realized that I had started to make the final turn too wide, misjudging the closeness of the telephone pole on my right. Visibility out my side windows was seriously limited by rain and fogging, probably caused by Romeo's heavy breathing a few miles back.

I advised the "pro" that I could not make the turn without hitting the car waiting for the stoplight in the opposite direction. The "pro" was convinced I could and said, "Give it the gas." We argued back and forth, and finally I acquiesced, gave it the gas, and hit the car at the corner.

We all headed to my house: the unremorseful "pro," the stunned family in the damaged car (I mean how often do a driver and passenger argue for five minutes and then hit you anyway?), and one shaky student driver, fearful that she might never be allowed behind the wheel again.

My father was livid to think that the "pro," who he was paying, could let an accident happen. I could see $$$ signs flashing in my dad's eyes as he worried about increased insurance premiums. The only thing worse than having a teenage driver on your policy is having one with a record.

I told my dad the whole story, and he complained to the "pro's" driving school first thing Monday morning and got the old "lech" fired. As for me, Dad knew the importance of getting behind the wheel again quickly after an accident before courage was lost. He recognized that I had been expected to do the almost impossible, i.e., turning that steering wheel with only one hand and without the benefit of power steering. He rectified the problem by getting power steering installed within one week. Two weeks later I passed my driving test. The state trooper who tested me paid my father a terrific compliment, saying he had never seen anyone handle a car so well with hand controls. That was only because he did not ask me to parallel park, a feat that remains a challenge. My dad loosened up a bit after the experience with the driving teacher and began to compare gray hairs and share war stories with the other dads in the neighborhood. He came to accept that teaching a teenage daughter with a disability to drive was no more or less nerve-wracking than teaching any teenager to drive.

I am able to treat the driving teacher's "pass" at me lightly in this essay because, fortunately for me, he did not aggressively pursue the matter when he saw I had no interest in him. For the record, I believe that adult sexual advances to a minor are unacceptable and in today's world meet the definition of sexual assault of a minor. All children and youth need to be prepared to deal with it should it happen to them. This was the second incident of this nature that occurred to me. The first, an elevator incident described in Chapter 6, happened when I was much younger, and it involved a male service provider. Again, fortunately for me, that man did not aggressively pursue the matter. In each instance, one of my parents reported the aggressor, and his employment was terminated.

Queen of the Prom

It was a long time between dates, from one encounter with a horny high school junior who was preying upon the quiet sophomore girls in search of an easy mark to a more mannerly young man who did not present himself until freshman year in college. Was I an easy mark? Possibly, but my perverse streak kicks in when I feel pressured, and in the case of the junior predator, I stopped him cold.

By the time my senior prom rolled around, I was no stranger to datelessness. It had become a way of life, and I wondered if this was how nuns got their start. Still, the prom was supposed to be the crowning event of one's high school career. Even the shy guys began to make eye contact and engage in brief conversations with girls as prom date neared. Herein lay much of the problem. It was the 1960s, prior to the feminist revolution, and hence the code of conduct passed from mother to daughter forbade a "nice" girl from asking a boy on a date. I was doomed by tradition and fine breeding!

Not that I didn't try to attract some male attention, mind you. I began by analyzing the problem and concluded that the major deterrent was my use of crutches. We can blame that one on the insurance industry. My parents were not able to obtain a life insurance policy for me until I was seventeen. We were told that I was considered high risk due to my use of crutches. Ha! It shows how little the insurance industry knew about assistive devices. I was much less of a risk using crutches than I was without them—more like a turtle than a sitting duck. At any rate, I reasoned that if my crutches were gone, not only could I be insured, but I could get a date for the prom, maybe with a future insurance agent, although they did not have a club for those at my high school.

I began by walking around my house without my crutches, then gradually used only one of them at school. Regardless of whether the new, less encumbered me was appealing to my male classmates, using only one crutch made getting to classes much easier. In three years, the scheduling geniuses at my school had rarely given me two classes in a row on the same floor, so I was constantly going up and down the stairs. With only one crutch, I could hang onto the railing, which made going up and down faster and less revealing. Yes, this was the age of the dress code, when girls still wore skirts or dresses to school. I often wondered what those at the bottom of the steps saw as I slowly made my way to the top. Whatever it was had not helped me in the dating department.

It soon became apparent that shedding my second crutch was going to be impossible as my stronger leg was not thriving with the extra demands on it. Try as I might, I knew I needed crutch support. My crutches and I had sort of a mechanical codependency.

As the prom date got closer and my indirect approach failed to produce any nibbles, I temporarily tossed aside tradition and fine breeding. I opted for a more direct tactic that placed me squarely in the 1990s, ahead of my time. I selected a likely candidate, i.e., an apparently shy boy without a girlfriend. My lucky prom "secret lotto winner" was a junior member of the basketball team. He was perfect—a studious young man who was not too tall, possibly a point guard. Best of all, his dad had a cool car that I would look great in on prom night. I studied his habits for a few weeks and when he didn't demonstrate any aberrant behavior, such as public spitting or nose-picking, I decided to breach the '60s' code of etiquette by calling him. It was at this point that my strategy began its spiral descent, stopping only a few steps before hell. In spite of my good intentions and directness, I was unable to identify myself in what became the first in a series of anonymous calls to this young man.

Had I been writing a romance novel, I could have salvaged this situation with our lovely heroine (moi) revealing her identity to this bespectacled Prince Charming at some secluded rendezvous spot on prom night. However, I had yet to formulate my management-by-procrastination strategy and after about a dozen calls, I jumped the gun by actually helping him to identify me in a game of Twenty Questions. We arranged to meet at his locker the next day. Alas, the rapport between us felt as hollow as an empty locker and our relationship ceased.

I spent prom night alone in my bedroom and learned one of life's most valuable lessons—treat special events, occasions, and holidays as any ordinary day, thereby keeping disappointment to a minimum. I danced alone to a few tunes on the radio that night, read a good book from my college-bound reading list, and turned in early, knowing that it would be hard for life's future disappointments to top this one, yet I had survived.

Discrimination 101—
An Introductory Course

Adulthood arrived without warning the day after I graduated from high school. It came after a night of modest celebration with a group of teetotaling aunts, uncles, and regular churchgoing friends, long before I had begun any wayward ways. It came in the form of an innocuous-looking envelope from the college of my choice which eventually became the college of my dreams.

The letter announced my freshman year living assignment, an address on Iron Street. Granted, mine had not been the most sophisticated approach to choosing a college, but I had been observant enough to notice there were no streets dissecting the campus. Therefore, I concluded that this house on Iron Street must be off campus.

I had been clear during my interview with the Dean of Admissions the previous December that I needed to live on campus. The dean advised me that although ninety-five percent of all freshmen were housed off campus, he would make note that I should be on campus. "No problem," he said.

The arrival of the infamous housing assignment letter was upsetting to me and almost the undoing of my mother. It stated to direct any housing questions to the Dean of Women, and my mother called her immediately.

Dean Emma Rae Stonewall was above all else a lady, fond of wearing white gloves and hosting teas. She was a product of her times, that is, the 1930s or '40s or maybe even the 1890s, ill-prepared for the incoming class of '69, which was comprised of budding feminists, future war protesters, and one short, tenacious person suddenly thrust into the role of disability activist. My mother, receiving no satisfaction from the dean, shoved the phone at me, whispering, "See if you can make her understand."

Among the dean's first comments was that if I could not handle the six block walk from Iron Street to campus, then I should not be going to college. Logic, obviously, was not one of the dean's strong suits. Instead of arguing the point, I reverted to an authority figure, the Dean of Admissions, and relayed his promise of an on-campus housing assignment. It worked! Dean Stonewall quickly ended our conversation, conferred with the Dean of Admissions, and called back to say she would move me to a dorm on campus, IF a vacancy became available during the summer. That vacancy materialized predictably in late August after one interim housing assignment, only three blocks from campus and down an even steeper hill.

I soon understood the rationale behind Dean Stonewall's incremental approach to placing me on campus. My new room was on the fourth floor of a condemned dormitory scheduled for demolition in a few years. The dean obviously wanted me to feel grateful for this problematic housing which I did—sort of. Determined to prove I had the "right stuff" to succeed at her latest initiation rite, I did not complain. My slow, multiple daily hikes up four flights of stairs did not go unnoticed by others living in the dorm. Word spread and soon Dean Stonewall was gaining a . . . reputation.

Dean Stonewall threw out one last hurdle before moving me to a modern dormitory with two working elevators. She approached me in the dining hall one evening accompanied by her entourage and stated she had received reports that I was using the condemned elevator in my dorm, which ended on the men's side of the fourth floor. I controlled my impulse, born out of nearly two weeks of climbing a million stairs, to scream, "What elevator?" for until that point, I was unaware there was a working elevator in the building. Within a week I was rewarded for my restraint with a room in one of the two new dorms.

The irony of the dean's steadfast adherence to the policy of housing all freshman off campus became apparent when the probationary freshmen, or "probies," as they were called, arrived for second semester. Eureka! The "probies" hit the jackpot. Not only did they become full-time students, they also were rewarded with rooms in one of the new dorms.

My relationship with Dean Stonewall became quite cordial over the next four years. As an officer of the Association of Resident Women, for which she served as an advisor, I was invited to tea in her apartment on several occasions and, of course, had to wear white gloves. Does anyone know how hard it is to hold onto crutch handles wearing cotton gloves? It's probably only second in difficulty to balancing a cup of red punch without spilling it on the white gloves while limping from the punchbowl to a chair. But these small sacrifices intended to keep the peace no doubt went unnoticed by the dean, a woman who never met a rule of etiquette she didn't like.

10

Off to College

Although choosing a college was not my strong suit, as evidenced by my essay "Discrimination 101," going to Bloomsburg State College, now Bloomsburg University, turned out to be a brilliant choice and marvelous experience. Being on my own and four hours away from family forced me to take charge of all aspects of my life, including my happiness. Choosing a school far from home was a deliberate strategy to prevent myself from being able to request a family rescue for anything other than a dire emergency. My freshman jitters and homesickness soon disappeared as I made new friends and joined activities.

Those few weeks I spent on the fourth floor of the condemned dormitory named Waller Hall were incredibly friend-producing, as it turned out. Nancy Strauss from the tiny town of Lansford, Pennsylvania was the first of these friends. One day she said, "Let's find a private place to sit and talk. I want to know all about you." We headed for the stairwell and talked for what seemed like hours. Her desire to know all about me included not being timid about asking disability-related questions. I confided in her and over time shared my fear about not being appealing to young men. As I recall, it went something like this following the loss of a promising boyfriend: "I'm sure I'll never get another date for the rest of my time in college." "Right," she replied with a skeptical look. Then, periodically she quoted me after seeing me talking with a new fellow.

Because Lansford was only an hour away from Bloomsburg, Nancy sometimes took me home with her on weekends. Her father owned a bar located at the front of their home. The available bar food was pizza and pierogis, which her mom prepared in their enormous kitchen. Nancy assisted whenever she was home, and I joined the busy kitchen when I visited.

Nancy was the first of my "gal pals," as my daughter now refers to them. Nancy's roommate, Glenanne Zeigenfuse, and two others from the fourth floor, Nancy Geiger and Chris Gruss, are also part of our group of six who have had several fun-filled reunions over the past fifty years. Boby Lou Cramer, who we met later, is the sixth.

Although I did not meet her until my sophomore year, Carol Berry lived on the third floor of Waller Hall during our freshman year and was well aware of my daily stair-climbing, as noted in "Discrimination 101." Carol and I were casual friends through membership in a service sorority. We bonded permanently in our senior year when we became roommates for six weeks.

Another enduring friendship happened my junior year when Polly Graybill joined us on the fourth floor of the new dorm, West Hall. Three years later, I was honored to be one of Polly's bridesmaids.

Academically, I continued to be an underachiever in college, yet I dedicated myself to courses in my major, Speech and Hearing Disorders, because the subject matter was fascinating, and I knew I must at least excel in my major. Otherwise, I concentrated on cultivating my social life. Pinochle was the game of choice at Bloomsburg, and I always was available for a game or, as I am fond of saying, I "minored" in pinochle. Knowing how to play pinochle proved to be a useful skill in adulthood when a neighborhood pinochle group formed in 1995 and is still going strong.

Bloomsburg U was at the top of a hill. I did considerable uphill walking but was young and as fit as I would ever be in my life. All went well until construction began for a new dorm my second year there. One rainy morning, the hill I needed to negotiate when returning to my dorm after class was a muddy mess. I inched along carefully, getting soaked in the process. Suddenly, my footing was gone and down I went! There I was, sitting in a huge puddle and covered with muddy splatter. My first collegiate "great fall" was one of my worst. Not only had it been witnessed by a crowd, but I could not get up, and once someone helped me to my feet, I resumed skidding and needed to be supported as I walked to dry pavement. Being completely powerless is a horrible feeling, especially for someone as independent as I always had been. I retreated, licked my wounds, and considered sequestering in a convent. My social circle was too strong to allow that to happen, however, and friends quickly drew me back into college life.

Finding a summer job after my first year of college proved impossible. Available opportunities mostly required considerable standing, walking, or physical skills I did not have. I suggested to my dad I could pump gas at the station owned by his friend. He just gave me a "look" that said "no daughter of mine . . . ," and I caved.

While I sulked, my mother decided it was time to call Ms. Grierson again. This time, my mother asked about a paying job at The Home the following summer. Ms. Grierson came to the rescue yet again! A job was created for me in the Speech and Language Department at The Home the summer after my sophomore year. It was a fabulous opportunity, and I learned as much there as I had in my first two years of college. I helped the Director of the Department with a variety of assignments. Most importantly, I was given the opportunity to work several times a day with a child who had autism. I spent every waking moment when I was not at work that summer reading about autism. Graduate students from the University of Pittsburgh were doing behavior modification with this child who was seldom verbal. I was assigned to see the child several times each day in a booth designed by autism expert O.I. Lovaas, MD, where I attempted to elicit verbalizations. I recorded every stimulus and response, or lack thereof, then provided the grad students with the data.

Dates and boyfriends were still rare during my first two years of college. In November of my third year, I met a freshman who was handsome, fun, and a Navy veteran taking advantage of the GI Bill. Perhaps being a little older than our classmates caused him to be secure enough to reach out to a girl with a disability.

It was 1969 when I graduated from college, and the women's movement was in its infancy. At the time, nice girls did not venture out on their own immediately after graduation. Not wanting to return home to my parents' tiny house, I rushed into marriage with this Navy veteran. We married three weeks after I graduated, though I realized after about two months it was a big mistake. Embarrassed to admit what I feared would be perceived as failure, I stuck with the marriage for seven years.

I've been lucky to maintain connections to several college friends. This group holds reunions every few years. Here we are in 2022. Behind me are Nancy Strauss Boos, Chris Gruss Ketz, Boby Cramer Huffard, Glenanne Zeigenfuse Farley, and kneeling in front is Nancy Geiger Smith.

PART 3

FINDING MY NICHE IN THIS WORLD

11

Launching My Career

My employment choices were limited by geography after college. Because my first husband had been in the military and still had two years of college to complete, we wanted to live in Bloomsburg; thus, I needed to find a job with a reasonable commute. I chose to work at a state-operated institution for people with intellectual disabilities about thirty miles away from Bloomsburg.

The institution, located in Selinsgrove, Pennsylvania, was a depressing place. Originally, it had been created for people with epilepsy, but once medications were developed to successfully control seizures for most people with epilepsy, the institution was re-purposed for people with intellectual disabilities.

My interview in the Speech and Hearing Department at Selinsgrove Center was on a bleak December day some six months prior to my start date. After the interview, one of the therapists, who had graduated from Bloomsburg the previous May, took me on a tour of the male wards in the central building. There were twelve large wards on each side of the main building with the cafeteria and professional offices in the middle. Each ward housed about fifty residents. Half walls separated the beds on either side from the middle of the room, which had been designed to be the activity area. Out of sight, each ward had a large group bathroom offering the residents little privacy. Our tour was moving along well, until we reached Central Male Unit 9, or CM-9, as it was called. Milling about were mostly young and naked men without any meaningful activity. The stench of urine and feces, which was scattered on the floor and smeared on the walls, was overpowering. Having never witnessed anything like this before, I stood transfixed for what seemed like a week. Finally, my former classmate, now my tour guide, tugged at my sleeve and said, "Let's move on." We did, but more than fifty years later, I've never forgotten what I saw. It was a defining moment that shaped my life as an advocate for people with intellectual and other developmental disabilities. Although I did not know about the burgeoning movement in Pennsylvania toward community services using three-person group homes, I knew that no human being belonged in the institution where I stood that day.

Since my car's battery had died that morning, my fiancé borrowed a fraternity brother's car and drove me to my interview. During my interview, he returned the borrowed car, then picked up mine with its new battery. I had a long wait for his return. Although there was a warm, comfortable seating area in the lobby of the building, I chose to stand in the chilly vestibule where there were no seats, wondering how I could even think of working in this place given what I had just witnessed.

Somehow, I did, though. Thanks to encouragement from my friend Polly Graybill, who had worked there the previous summer and whose mother was an RN and the Director of Training at Selinsgrove Center, I was able to overcome my revulsion for the place. By the time I arrived, they had used behavior modification to create a better living environment on CM-9.

I worked at Selinsgrove Center for three years and loved the numerous residents with whom I had contact. Since we were a friendly, fun-loving bunch in the Speech and Hearing Department, some of the residents who had jobs in the kitchen or cafeteria stopped by to visit nearly every day, and our offices reminded me of a TV sitcom with a regular cast of characters. We truly enjoyed each other's company.

There were approximately 1,600 residents at this state institution when I began working there.

Some deinstitutionalization was underway, though it was happening slowly. My job was to provide mostly language therapy, as well as to do speech and language evaluations for people being newly admitted. Given the enormity of this facility, our department was able to assist only a small fraction of those who needed us.

While I liked all the Selinsgrove residents with whom I had contact, I adored one little girl I'll call Deedee. She was five years old when I arrived, and I saw her every day for language therapy. She melted my heart. One day, Deedee came to therapy with a big lump in her abdominal area covered by her dress. I asked if I could see what it was, she said yes, and I lifted her dress. This child was wearing size-six ladies' underwear that the staff had knotted in front so they would not fall down. Faster than you can say, "Where's the nearest shopping center?" I used this as an excuse to buy Deedee a new wardrobe and raced to a nearby shopping plaza after work. I also picked up a laundry marking pen to inscribe her name, hoping there might be at least a slim chance the clothes would be returned to her after traveling to the laundry center.

I began working on my M.Ed. in speech and language disorders during my third year at Selinsgrove. By this time, I lived in an apartment above the hardware store on Main Street in downtown Selinsgrove. Amish farmers would tie their buggies to the posts in the parking lot behind the store where I also parked, and their wives sold baked goodies, fruits, and vegetables across the street every Saturday morning. The town had a charming atmosphere. I spent much time that year traveling to and from Bloomsburg for evening and summer classes and devoted most of my discretionary time to studying and writing papers. Finally, I became a good student!

In late June 1972, my final year in Selinsgrove, Hurricane Agnes dumped a voluminous amount of rain on central and northeastern Pennsylvania, causing massive flooding up and down the Susquehanna Valley. Much of the workforce at the institution lived on the opposite side of the Susquehanna River from Selinsgrove. During this weather crisis, all bridges were closed, and they could not get to work. There was a desperate need for volunteers to help on the wards. Of course, I volunteered even though I could not do some of the work, such as lifting and bathing. I found plenty of other tasks I was able to undertake, including changing diapers, and assisting people to eat, brush their teeth, and get dressed. I slept on a cot in the basement at night and rushed home at least three times a day to let my dog out and feed her.

My responsibilities in this first job grew and by my final performance evaluation, I had been identified for a future leadership position. Giving credit where it is due, my first husband, a business major, had shared with me some words of wisdom he paraphrased from management guru Peter Drucker: "Always take on jobs that no one else wants to do and you'll be noticed." When no one offered to teach some basic sign language to ward personnel, I volunteered even though I was still learning it myself. When someone was needed to speak at the orientation of new personnel who would work on the wards, I raised my hand.

At my exit conference, the director of the department disclosed that the superintendent of the institution had advised her not to hire me due to my disability. He was an old-school physician working beyond the typical retirement age. He reasoned that I could not walk repeatedly each day to the wards to bring the residents to therapy in our department. The context for her reporting this to me was how happy she was that she did not take his advice, though I still wonder if I was hired because there were no other candidates for the job at the time. Her remarks provided me with my first glimpse of employment discrimination. And, by the way, I walked repeatedly to the wards each day to bring my young clients to and from therapy. Since I did not walk rapidly, it meant that we got to know each other better and, often, some therapy occurred in the hallways as we applied what was being learned in therapy to an everyday setting.

Leaving Selinsgrove State Center after three years was easy, except for saying goodbye to Deedee. I returned to visit her a few times, and when I said my final goodbye before moving to Maryland, she was a teenager. I still think of her often and cherish the memories of my time spent with her and the many likeable residents at Selinsgrove. Hopefully, she and many others got the chance to move to and enjoy community living in the ensuing years.

12

Discovering My Purpose

I left Selinsgrove after three years when my first husband completed college and found a job in Scranton, Pennsylvania. In the words of the biblical Ruth, "Whither thou goest." My next job was as a speech and language therapist in the Wilkes-Barre Area School District, thanks to being recruited by a supervisor whom I had met in grad school at Bloomsburg.

Being a public-school therapist in 1972 meant that I was itinerant, providing therapy at multiple schools each week. I was assigned to four schools chosen for me because of my experience with people having intellectual disabilities. At each of my schools I had a mix of students who did not have intellectual disabilities and saw me for articulation therapy, such as correcting lisps and distorted "r" sounds, as well as students with intellectual disabilities who needed a combination of articulation and language therapy. Having worked with individuals with intellectual disabilities at

Selinsgrove Center for three years, I knew I could have little impact with those children in the public schools. They needed therapy three times each week optimally, whereas I could see them only once a week due to a large caseload.

At the time, P.L. 94-142, now called the Individuals with Disabilities Education Act (IDEA) had not been enacted. Speech and language therapists in Pennsylvania's public schools were expected to close a certain percentage of cases each school year. Therapy with students not having intellectual disabilities was a breeze. They responded well, made rapid improvements, and usually were discharged within one school year; hence they dominated my caseload. Once P.L. 94-142 became law, greater emphasis was given to students with more significant disabilities.

As an itinerant therapist, I had no permanent workspace and needed to carry all materials and supplies with me. My car quickly began to resemble the back-to-school section of an office supply store. Since walking was always a challenge under ideal circumstances, walking while carrying my materials into each school, most of which had stairs, was a "great fall" waiting to happen. My creative supervisor suggested asking the principal at each school to identify a responsible sixth-grader to serve as a sherpa. The students met me at my car each morning I was at their school and at the end of classes. Remarkably, the kids who volunteered were quite reliable.

My employment at Selinsgrove had been twelve months versus ten months now that I was working in a public school system. What to do with two months of vacation? It was the summer of 1973 and life was relatively simple then. No children. No home ownership projects. Hmmm, how could I make my summer both interesting and meaningful?

I scanned the Yellow Pages and contacted the local United Cerebral Palsy (UCP) affiliate in Scranton where I lived to see if they needed a volunteer. A lovely woman interviewed me, and we agreed that I would assist their adults with ceramics, rug hooking, and decoupage two afternoons each week. It did not take long for me to recognize something was very wrong with this picture. Here I was at age twenty-four helping people nearly twice my age with arts and crafts. While I found crafting a pleasant diversion from grad school and my job, this was how the adults with cerebral palsy spent their days. How was it that their lives were so different than mine? Was this how the girl who had accompanied me for surgery all those years ago now spent her days?

During this summer gig, I watched the Executive Director come and go, probably to meetings outside of their building. One evening over dinner, I said to my first husband, "I want her job. I could really change that center for the people they serve." While I had no specifics in mind at the time, I knew the lives of the participants could be more fulfilling.

My husband mentioned my desire to direct the UCP chapter to one of his colleagues who licensed such programs. Fast-forward to spring 1974 and this colleague approached him saying, "If your wife really wants to direct a UCP affiliate, tell her the one in Wilkes-Barre is looking for a new Executive Director." She then added the caveat, "But also tell her that it's about to go under." The value of having a spouse with a good job meant that I was free to take a chance on this job if I wanted, and I did. After two interviews, the second with a national UCP staff member present, I was hired. Panic struck on my drive home when I realized one of my responsibilities was to prepare budgets. "No big deal," said my husband with the degree in business administration when I shared my fear, "budgeting is just a guesstimate." And, thus, I slept soundly that night.

What I found at this UCP affiliate, some twenty miles south of the one in Scranton where I had volunteered the previous summer, was much the same, i.e., adults transported daily on one of three vehicles, in various states of dysfunction, to do arts and crafts. Even worse, some of their mothers occasionally would hop on the bus and ask for a special stop at the mall where they could shop.

Having never undertaken organizational change before, I plunged in without really engaging the families. Their views of their "children" had been developed and reinforced over many years as a result of public-school systems that did not welcome, nor include them. It is a rare person who can learn and succeed without consistent formal schooling, and these adults were the products of systemic educational discrimination that occurred prior to the 1970s.

Change happened at this UCP affiliate. We initiated residential services and hired a recreational staffer who connected people with community activities and often with volunteers who shared their interests. Our day program participants went to activities in the community in small groups at least once a week. We began an advocacy group and involved them in meetings with the county's para-transit coordinator, who was just starting that service. The parents gradually let go and the adults with disabilities began to experience more freedom and to dream, at least a little bit. While I remained unpopular with the parents, some acknowledged that greater independence for their sons and daughters would prepare them for the future once the parents were gone.

Although the mothers were not sympathetic to the need for changes being made, my board of directors could not have been stronger and more supportive. They were a group of mostly professional men in their late twenties and thirties. My vision for the organization was steeped in respect for those we served, and I possessed the ability to execute an enormous workload. My highly engaged board members, led by Marshall Jacobson, Esq., were actively involved in committees. Every week at least one board committee held an evening meeting. Of course, I attended them all and learned much from this stellar group, including how to be more tactful. My "bull in a china shop" approach to organizational change was tempered, and I learned to better analyze situations, involve stakeholders early and often, and be more reflective.

Overall, my time with UCP in Wilkes-Barre was successful and good changes happened. In addition to absorbing wisdom from my talented and dedicated board members, the fine trainings and conferences provided by the national UCP organization were packed with sessions on best practices, as well as after-hour opportunities to pick the brains of the presenters and my colleagues from other UCP affiliates.

This period of my life was personally and professionally fulfilling. I gained confidence in my abilities and began to realize my vision of improving the quality of life for others with disabilities.

13

Times Were Changing

My employment with UCP in Wilkes-Barre, Pennsylvania spanned from 1974 to 1979. During this same period, truly remarkable changes were happening across the United States. Vietnam veterans, many of whom had sustained permanent disabilities, were returning home, and the women's movement was transforming the aspirations of women throughout the country. An upheaval in my personal life occurred in 1976 when my marriage ended. Although the divorce was my decision, it nevertheless was quite upsetting. Like so many other young women of my era, I had gone from my parents' home to college, then on to marriage three weeks after graduation. With the divorce, I found myself completely responsible for every aspect and detail of my life. Shared decision-making was history. Revisiting the saying I'd learned the night of my prom, "What doesn't kill you makes you stronger," I threw myself further into my work, finished my thesis, and, voilà!, my strength increased.

While I had a vision of inclusion for the people we served at UCP, I did not identify as a disability activist, nor did I see a revolution coming. My eyes were opened in 1976 when I attended the Pennsylvania Governor's Conference on the Handicapped, a precursor to the White House Conference on the Handicapped.

While participating at the Pennsylvania conference, I learned of a dozen or more local grassroots advocacy groups comprised of people with mostly mobility disabilities who were advocating for architectural accessibility. These groups had names such as Operation Overcome, a group from Allentown, Pennsylvania, and Disabled in Action from Philadelphia. Very cool people were members of these groups, and I wondered where they had been hiding and why I'd not seen them as I traveled around the state. The absence of accessibility in the built environment explained their invisibility. Most of these local activists used wheelchairs, while I still walked. Inaccessible buildings and communities were an inconvenience for me but an absolute barrier for them. The members of these groups were well informed about issues of accessibility, and many had been advocating with local authorities for curb cuts, accessible transportation, and reserved parking. In retrospect, I wonder if these local Pennsylvania groups were aware of the historic independent living movement that had been launched by Ed Roberts in Berkeley, California in 1972. Without the benefit of the internet or social media, information traveled slowly and was dependent on presentations and, more likely, after-hours conversations during conferences. Traditional media coverage was infrequent at best.

Section 504 of the 1973 Rehabilitation Act became the first civil rights law for people with disabilities. In 1977, disability activists held sit-ins at federal buildings to force the signing of regulations to implement Section 504. The San Francisco sit-in led by Judy Heumann lasted a remarkable twenty-six days. The ink was barely dry on the Section 504 regulations when the Pennsylvania Developmental Disabilities Council funded the Public Interest Law Center of Philadelphia to conduct training for people with disabilities in Philadelphia and Pittsburgh. Jim Raggio was one of the trainers, as was the dynamic Tom Gilhool, who had been the lead attorney in Pennsylvania's right to education lawsuit resulting in the PARC consent decree. The decree was the precursor to PL 94-142, the Education of All Handicapped Children Act, now known as the Individuals with Disabilities Education Act.

I traveled to Philadelphia for the Section 504 training. During the first plenary session, Tom and Jim taught us the content of the law. Tom pranced around the stage and balanced precariously on the back of a chair. Jim's delivery was not nearly as animated but equally informative. We then broke into groups where we role-played in assigned scenarios with "faux officials," learning to support our arguments for access to buildings and programs with key sections of the regulations. Suddenly, during this training, I had an epiphany. These Section 504 regulations would have solved my collegiate housing problem with Dean Stonewall. The concept of "reasonable accommodation" could have been used to grant me a room in a dorm with a working elevator when housing assignments originally were being made, rather than my having to endure the dean's incremental approach. Section 504 was impressive. Progress was being made and it would be life-changing for many people.

The success of the Philadelphia training prompted the Pennsylvania Developmental Disabilities Council to fund more 504 training throughout the state. In the fall, I had a call from my counterpart at UCP of Philadelphia saying that he had recommended me to Jim Raggio, who was seeking a logistical coordinator for the Northeastern Pennsylvania training. Jim and I spoke by phone many times as the training plans fell into place. Jim later said I impressed him with my competence, and he imagined me to be much older. Jim's deep commitment to using the law to improve access for people with disabilities was apparent throughout our conversations. We met in person for the first time over dinner the evening before the Northeast Pennsylvania training. I was enamored. Then, as suddenly as he had arrived in Wilkes-Barre, he left.

A few months later, I was invited by a friend from Operation Overcome to join him for a debriefing with Jim, who was developing more 504 training under a new contract with the former US Department of Health, Education and Welfare for thirteen states and territories. No fireworks went off, though I remained smitten.

More time passed, then I was asked to speak at a conference in Harrisburg in mid-July over a weekend. Not relishing the idea of working yet another weekend, I stalled a bit by asking what the conference program looked like and who else would be speaking. When I heard Jim's name, I immediately agreed. As it turned out, Jim's approach had been similar, and he committed to speak when he learned they were inviting me. The following essay, "My Destiny," captures the magic of that weekend and the beginning of our lifetime relationship.

My Destiny

As the saying goes, "Neither rain nor snow nor gloom of night . . . can keep the letter carrier from his/her appointed rounds." Neither can a great fall and a bruised tailbone deter a young woman from fulfilling her destiny.

Most of my great falls, while memorable, have been relatively harmless, injuring only my dignity. There was one, however, that could have altered the course of history, or at least my family tree. It happened in the bathroom, and the cause was the peculiar effect of overexerting my few working leg muscles in a pool the previous day.

I paid for this silliness in the bathroom the next morning. My knee buckled from the previous day's workout and I came crashing down, clipping my tailbone on the edge of the tub. I lay and sat on ice packs that day and by the next morning pronounced myself well enough to meet My Destiny.

I had agreed to give up another precious weekend to speak at a conference knowing that My Destiny would be speaking there as well. We had met on prior occasions, and I sometimes had a vision of myself with gray hair sitting next to him while knitting booties for our grandchild.

The greatest challenge of this weekend conference was traveling there. Ordinarily, it was a two-hour drive, but I managed to double it by stopping at every rest stop and scenic overlook on the interstate in order to stand and move, temporarily removing pressure on my tailbone.

There was no sign of My Destiny before or during dinner or at the first plenary session that evening. I retired to the bar and chose a table with a view of the door. He arrived shortly after I had perched precariously on my injured tush. He scanned the room, obviously looking for someone. Me, I concluded. As it turned out, this was an unspoken, though mutual, attraction, and he joined me as soon as our eyes met. Since I couldn't sit still for more than a few minutes, the conversation turned to my reason for fidgeting, i.e., the great fall and my injured tailbone. While the word "fall" would have been enough to make most men choke on their beer and signal for the bill, My Destiny saw an opportunity and suggested we go to a nearby hotel with a Jacuzzi. He had stayed there recently while speaking at another conference. Once a guest, always a guest!

Never mind that neither of us were paying customers at the nearby hotel, we strolled authoritatively through the lobby and into the courtyard, where I gingerly lowered myself into the Jacuzzi's warm and bubbling water.

If there was something we, the lovestruck, did not want that night, it was company. Conversation is difficult enough on a first date without adding a stranger to the mix. Nevertheless, a lady, perhaps in her early fifties, strolled by in her street clothes and paused to chat with us. She found us fascinating and enjoyed the "chemistry between us" (her words) so much that, instead of leaving us alone to cultivate that chemistry, she joined us—without bothering to change into a bathing suit. She was giddy at the thought of losing her inhibitions and the reality of trying to tame her ballooning skirt, which, thanks to the churning water, behaved like a parachute. She kept repeating, "If only my husband could see me, he wouldn't believe it." During a moment when she was seriously into skirt management, My Destiny and I exchanged a glance that more or less implored her husband to come out on the balcony, express shock, and retrieve her. The way our luck was running that night, though, he probably would have joined us.

Our giggling friend stayed until we finally called it quits. In retrospect, it was an entertaining first date for all three of us.

My Destiny and I found plenty of quiet, uninterrupted time in the next few years that more than made up for the first date. Once we had children, we often laughed about that first date in the Jacuzzi and how it was a preview of the incredible lack of privacy that every couple with children endures. And, as for my great fall leading into that weekend? At least this time, a little suffering paid off.

14

The Beginning of My Best Life

The romance that began during the magical weekend conference in Harrisburg has turned into a forty-plus-year marriage. The courtship phase was not without a few bumps created by my insecurities, though. Well aware that fifty percent of all marriages end in divorce, I allowed an insidious little creature inside my head to convince me I might be a loser who could not achieve long-term success in the relationship realm. Jim, exhibiting his amazing patience and usual optimism, pointed out that half of all marriages succeed. He calmed me and convinced me that he was different from the average fella and that I should relax and enjoy our relationship. Fortunately, I heeded.

At the time of our marriage, society was in the transition phase from women bearing all responsibilities on the home front to couples sharing home and childcare tasks. Progressive men who viewed marriage as a full partnership were still in short supply. Luckily, I found an enlightened man in Jim Raggio, who was willing to pull his share of the load or even more. Was I able to pull fifty percent of the load? Absolutely! Considering all I could do with or without adaptations, then throw in a few extras such as being able to sew window treatments, and I was a treasure waiting to be discovered.

In the middle of our first year as a couple, I moved to Maryland for a job with another United Cerebral Palsy affiliate. I had been looking for a new opportunity in the Philadelphia area where Jim lived and worked but was having no luck. A UCP board member from Prince George's County, Maryland knew of my work in Wilkes-Barre and recruited me to move south. And just like that, I became a Marylander.

Jim and I were married in March 1980. My concern about the embarrassment of a possible second failed marriage manifested itself in the search for a wedding dress. My first marriage had featured the beautiful gown and all the wedding trappings of a church ceremony and reception. For the second occasion, I searched in three states for a lovely dress, though not a wedding gown, and finally settled on an ordinary two-piece dress that would have been more appropriate for work than on my wedding day. I cringe a bit when looking at the photos from that day but accept it as an indicator of my much-needed personal growth.

We did not invite our families to the wedding since my father was ill and unable to travel. Jim's best friend, David Keller, and one of my college roommates, Carol Berry Shumaker, were our attendants. Carol's husband Ian was the fifth participant.

Without the expense of a wedding, we excitedly scheduled a two-week honeymoon in Mexico. The essay, Olé, describes our honeymoon adventures and my first trip outside the US. Other than my recuperation from orthopedic surgery as a child, the first time I used a wheelchair was on my honeymoon. It was a convenience, given the amount of walking we were doing.

Jim and I on our wedding day

Olé

Most couples plan their honeymoons with nothing more than romance on their minds. Not us. My husband, the Italian version of Indiana Jones, booked our wedding trip into that most frequented of honeymoon getaways, Mexico City. That's right, Mexico City, with its reputation for "tummy troubles," poor air quality, and a population then in excess of fifteen million, all of whom seemed to drive colorful vintage Volkswagens. We were destined for adventure!

Had it not been for a last-minute tip from a recent visitor to Mexico City, a state auditor, grateful for the fun time he was having dissecting my nonprofit's financial records from a few years prior to my arrival, we would have stayed at a hotel that had only twin beds. In the nick of time, we changed reservations to the Continental Hotel with a room facing the most exciting of all Mexican spectacles—the intersection of the Zocala and Reforma, two of the busiest streets in the world. When we arrived on a Sunday afternoon, all was relatively quiet, offering no hint of what awaited us the next morning.

A major lowlight of our trip to Mexico City was adjusting to the high altitude, whose effects I began to feel soon after our plane landed. While my husband set off on his first adventure to buy tickets to the renowned Folklore Ballet, I chose to stay at the hotel to elevate my feet which, by that time, looked like I was wearing two pairs of sweat socks under my skin. Fluid retention, dang.

My new and better half returned with tickets for seats in the balcony offering a "wonderful view" of this dancing extravaganza—only you had to be part mountain goat to get to them. In the process of climbing the steep stairs with no hand railing, I became reacquainted with my fear of heights. Considering the number of "great falls" I've taken, an occasional panic attack is not out of order, and I indulged myself in one as soon as I turned around and noticed that the seat in front of mine was at my foot level—as in, nothing to break a fall. My compliments go to the Mexican architects and engineers who knew how to construct an auditorium with all seats having an unimpeded view of the stage. The Folklore Ballet was magnificent, and my adventure of getting to and from my seat proved to be valuable training for the week ahead, specifically pyramid climbing.

Our initial mistake was going to sleep with the sliding glass door open our first night, but since we were on the tenth floor in a room with iron fencing outside the sliding door rather than a balcony, it seemed a safe bet that no intruder would scale the building to enter our room. The horn honking began promptly at 7:00 a.m. on Monday and every weekday morning. This assault on our eardrums as the commuters approached our intersection reached a crescendo by 8:00 a.m. It was deafening. Hundreds of brightly colored little Volkswagens crept forward under our window. The drivers aimed their cars in all directions as they jockeyed for precious inches of roadway or even curbs. Horn honking seemed to be an economical Mexican substitute for mental health services, literally a "sound" way to express one's frustrations.

We realized on the second morning that having the sliding glass doors closed made little difference, and by the third morning we made a serious attempt at lip reading. If this is beginning to sound like an atypical honeymoon, consider the old adage, "early to bed and early to rise" and you will understand how we coped.

My husband, who learned to drive in New York City and can hold his own on the Long Island Expressway with the most aggressive drivers, took one look at the traffic and announced we would forego renting a car. That left us with four options: public buses, the subway, cabs, and peseros, which are taxis that travel a fixed route up and down the Reforma.

Even from ten stories up, it was apparent that buses were not a feasible option. Every seat and inch of floor space was occupied to the point where the driver could barely close the door, and passengers leaned out the windows in order to breathe.

We began with cabs. As any Mexico City travel guide explains, the passenger must negotiate a price with the cab driver before going for a ride. Since the Mexican cab drivers had much better command of Spanish than we did and made sport out of haggling over the cost with tourists, we were soon paying top price for cab rides and blowing our budget.

The last straw came at the end of a pesero ride from the Anthropological Museum to our hotel. Peseros charge a set fee per passenger and make frequent stops to pick up and discharge people, thereby always ensuring a full vehicle. By Mexican standards, the back seat of a pesero should accommodate four people. This would have been quite a feat under normal circumstances, but, just our luck, an exceptionally tall, big-boned German woman joined us in the back seat. Her equally gigantic husband nearly squeezed to death a slightly built Mexican man and the driver in the front. Did they get charged extra for being so big? Of course not. When it was time for us to pay, however, the driver pointed to my crutches and stated the price of three passengers. My husband objected and we understood the driver to say that he usually stuffed four passengers in the back seat, but because of my crutches our voyage only had three. Although I had contained my crutches between my knees to make room for Brunhilde, we did not wish to be "ugly Americans" and paid for an extra person without creating a scene.

The pesero driver may have won that battle, but he lost the war. In retaliation for this incident, we set off in search of our own wheels. We intended to rent a wheelchair, but when we inquired about rental places at the hotel's front desk, they presented us with a loaner. This sorry-looking piece of equipment was not a wheelchair to compete with in Paralympic events, nor even one that I would dare to be seen in back home, but since I didn't know anyone in Mexico City, I used it—after we cleaned it up. It appeared that someone had lost their lunch all over the chair, and I soon understood how that could happen as my husband pushed me rapidly along the sidewalk over large cracks and small craters left by the most recent earthquake. I hung on for dear life and vowed not to eat or drink for the remainder of our trip. Between guilt feelings over seeing women and children begging in the streets and the effects of the bumpy rides, I was destined to become skinny if only I could stay in Mexico City long enough.

No trip to Mexico City is complete without a visit to the Teotihuacan pyramids. On our third day, we boarded a small tour bus with a family of four and headed out of town to see these wondrous structures. Although six passengers would qualify this bus as a "high occupancy vehicle" in Washington, DC, having empty seats felt sinfully wasteful by Mexican standards.

Not knowing what to expect at the pyramids, we dragged along the borrowed wheelchair. No sooner had we arrived than a girl about nine years old approached us and offered to trade a trinket for the wheelchair. We laughed good-naturedly and said, "No, thank you." Not to be rebuffed easily, this young businesswoman tagged along, bargaining for the chair, my crutches, and our camera in exchange for the paltry contents of her pockets. She finally gave up and bartered with a group of new arrivals.

After we poked around the ancient structures near the entrance, the driver offered to take us to the end. Adventurous fools that we were, we politely declined in favor of walking.

The brochure photos of the pyramids were deceptive. There appeared to be a single pyramid having two large sets of stairs on either side. Once we climbed the first set of stairs, we were stunned to discover there were numerous pyramids with a large field between each. Instead of turning back, we plodded on. Someday when I'm old, lying in bed in a nursing home, I will reflect on abusing my body going up and down and up and down the steps of the pyramids. My husband made like Sisyphus dragging the wheelchair up and down and across the field, only to be rewarded with more of the same. By the midpoint, he would have given the wheelchair willingly to that young barterer we met at the entrance, then reimbursed the hotel for its loss.

Being carefree newlyweds, though, we laughed and joked about our situation and how amazed our driver and traveling companions would be when we finished our long trek and arrived at the finish line. Not that this was a race, mind you. Actually, we took so long, it's a wonder they didn't send out a search party. But arrive we did, only we were the ones who were surprised, not our companions. For there, at the end, scarfing down tacos and enjoying the early evening breezes, was a tour group of about twenty wheelchair users, all of whom looked rested and perplexed as this worn-out and dusty camper hiked the last few steps before collapsing into the beat-up old wheelchair. Exhausted, yes, but loving every minute of my exotic Mexican vacation!

PART 4
ON A MISSION

15

Such a Good Use of Our Tax Dollars!

A few months after returning from my honeymoon, I changed jobs, leaving UCP and becoming the Associate Director of the Maryland Developmental Disabilities Council (DD Council). After three years there, I was named Executive Director. The Council jobs were my all-time favorites. Working with the forty members appointed by the governor to change systems of service for people with intellectual and developmental disabilities was a rare privilege. The Council membership, outlined in federal law, is dominated by parents and people with disabilities who are joined by state agency representatives, advocates, and service providers. Council meetings create a forum for fascinating discussions and the honest exchange of ideas and opinions from this group with diverse experiences and perspectives.

Having funding for demonstration projects designed to influence the changes desired by Council members gives DD Councils high visibility and power. Each year we developed requests for proposals (RFPs) and awarded over a half million dollars for a variety of activities. State DD Councils can and should make bold statements with their funding to shape attitudes and change the status quo. They are forward thinking and constantly stay on the cutting edge.

Attendant Care

One of my first major assignments from Phil Holmes, Executive Director of the DD Council who had recruited and hired me, was to shepherd a piece of legislation through the Maryland General Assembly. Phil was clear from the outset that he wanted me to inherit his job after three years. "It's time," he said, "for you to learn the legislative process. You'll need to know it when you become Executive Director." Two advocates with significant physical disabilities came to us asking for our help in securing passage of a bill that would provide financial assistance to people who require attendant care. In spite of their best efforts, the bill had failed twice and was on the verge of becoming a perennial loser. Neither of these proponents had much experience in the legislative arena but sensed the open window of opportunity might close soon. Although a greenhorn myself, I had time to devote to the endeavor and expert coaching from Phil.

The bill's sponsor, Senator Art Helton, was surprised by the small amount of interest and support generated for the bill each time it had been introduced. Together, we made changes to strengthen the bill, and it became the only program within state government that provided cash reimbursement to the person with a disability for their attendant care. We decided to have a companion bill introduced in the House of Delegates. At Senator Helton's suggestion, I found a House sponsor who had not introduced disability legislation previously. The late Lorraine Sheehan agreed to be the House sponsor, and I later learned her interest stemmed from having a son with a disability. Lorraine became my legislative mentor and did the same for many other disability advocates in the ensuing years.

An important step was to build support for the legislation from other advocates with an interest in creating an Attendant Care Program in our state. Although there was not an organized disability rights movement in Maryland at the time, there were several groups eager to write letters and make phone calls to elected officials in support of the Attendant Care bill. My job was to keep them apprised of its status through regular updates and action alerts.

Senator Helton was grateful for my involvement and arranged for me to do a lengthy presentation to the Finance Committee about the need for and content of the bill and my research on other states' programs. Miraculously and despite my on-the-job learning, the bill passed. The Attendant Care Program continues today, more than forty years later.

Family Supports

During my time at the Maryland DD Council, we established family support services to assist families with children who had developmental disabilities. As a new parent myself at the time, I believed Family Support Services to be among the most noble causes. Parents who have a child with a developmental disability must navigate a world of healthcare professionals and the special education system while learning the rules and developing strategies to secure the services, supports, and accommodations that will enable their child with a disability to succeed. Phew! If that's not overwhelming enough, they must do it all while dealing with the usual parental challenges. Providing them with funding for respite care and other services or products such as special formula or diapers, makes their lives just a little easier.

Someone once introduced me at a meeting as the "mother of family support services." The woman who conceptualized this program, though, was Renee Dixon, one of the parent members of the DD Council. Renee lived in rural St. Mary's County and had a son with multiple disabilities who required round-the-clock assistance. With her wry sense of humor and clear, and pointed, communication skills, Renee was well liked by her fellow Council members, and particularly effective in conversations with the DD Council's state agency representatives.

Renee would share stories about her son and how families like hers should have access to respite care or financial help to pay for items or services needed throughout their lives. She lobbied the other members of the DD Council, before or after a meeting, to support a large RFP for family support services. They agreed and we began a demonstration project in 1983 with five service providers. The projects had just begun when Phil resigned, and I became the Acting Director of the DD Council. While "Acting" I could not hire a permanent employee to fill my vacant position; hence I hired a temporary contractual employee, Robin Shaivitz, who had been Delegate Lorraine Sheehan's legislative aide. Hiring Robin was invaluable. She had extensive knowledge of both the legislative process and the members of our General Assembly. Together Robin and I drafted legislation to make the Family Support Services Program permanent within state government once the DD Council funding ended. Robin found a committed legislator to sponsor the bill and did the necessary behind-the-scenes educating of members of the Finance Committee, to which the bill was assigned, on the importance and value of Family Support Services. Our bill passed the first year it was introduced. Renee Dixon's vision and determination has enabled thousands of Maryland families to receive assistance and has made their lives just a little easier.

Supported Employment

In 1987, the Office of Special Education and Rehabilitation Services (OSERS), located within the US Department of Education, issued a request for proposals for states to create systems change moving away from funding sheltered workshops and work activity centers where people were paid a pittance to a new system of providing supports for people in real jobs to ensure their success.

A group of key agencies in Maryland had begun meeting six months in advance of this highly anticipated RFP. A member of this group, Jim Gardner, director of what was then known as the University Affiliated Program at Kennedy-Krieger Institute, volunteered me to chair the small grant-writing team, and we commenced as soon as the RFP was issued. We were joined by Michael Smull, then working at the University of Maryland in Baltimore, and one of our DD Council staff, Kimberly Riddle. The four of us devoted countless hours over the next six weeks writing the grant and obtaining commitments from service providers who agreed to move people from sheltered workshops to real jobs. Further, we engaged two private foundations that offered to supplement federal funding if Maryland became a chosen state. One foundation granted funds to develop a video for parents to increase their understanding and comfort with supported employment. The second funded our data collection. Our proposal was selected by OSERS and, over the next five years, Maryland exceeded all goals we had set for ourselves.

When a new governor came to office in 1988, we wanted to introduce him to supported employment to gain his support of our efforts, particularly with outreach to employers. He had a fully equipped bus for his trips around the state, and we arranged a bus tour to several supported employment sites. Although I had suggested this whirlwind bus tour, I could not participate in the valuable conversation with the governor on board, for the bus was not wheelchair accessible. Sadly, I trailed behind in my car and trusted those on board to convey our messages accurately. We needed to depict how jobs empowered people with developmental disabilities, and, apparently, we succeeded as the governor was impressed with what he saw and heard.

During my time at the DD Council, we awarded funds for numerous activities to promote the expansion of family support services, supported employment, and inclusive education. Through grants, legislative advocacy, conferences, publications, and deliberations at many, many meetings, the DD Council has helped Maryland progress from a state that relied upon institutions to one that is dominated by community-based supports.

Once the Council promoted me as Executive Director in 1984, our work was enhanced by the dedication of Associate Director Rick Glaser, then when Rick left, Susanne Elrod. With our talented staff and visionary Council members, we accomplished much during my six years as Executive Director.

In my opinion the federal Developmental Disabilities Act that created DD Councils and their sister organizations, the State Protection and Advocacy agencies and the University Centers for Excellence in Developmental Disabilities, is one of the most brilliant pieces of legislation enacted by Congress. It has been the basis for creating a system within each state of community-based supports and services for people with the most significant disabilities. Many states, including Maryland, have used the DD Act to develop greater capacity within the community and then been propelled through the values within the DD Act to close state institutions. The Developmental Disabilities Act is a shining example of how our federal taxes work to produce better lives for Americans with disabilities.

The Press Conference

There is no quicker way of adding drama to a dignified event than with a great fall. And people wonder how I've stayed humble all my life!

The dignified event was a press conference staged by the Maryland Developmental Disabilities Council, the small state agency for which I worked. The cabinet secretaries of five departments within state government were to be presented with a report from individuals with disabilities and families who had contributed to it. We had invited media coverage, since this marked the first time that high-level department heads had met with and heard directly from people affected by the services their agencies delivered, or possibly did not, but should be offering.

In addition to the secretaries and their key program directors, there were about seventy-five people in the audience. I was to act as emcee and fully intended to maintain a low profile. Making a good impression was important, though, since I was still Acting Director of this little agency and wanted the job permanently. Some members of the Search Committee who would make the hiring decision were present. My ability to be taken seriously as an advocate and negotiator with the various state agencies was also at stake on this particular day.

Although by this time I was an experienced administrator, I was still young in comparison to the secretaries and their program directors and oh so naïve. Case in point. One morning shortly after the grand coronation of the new Secretary of the Health Department, she and I rode on the elevator together. There we were, she with two briefcases stuffed with paperwork that she undoubtedly labored over until after midnight and me with a paper bag full of zucchini from my garden to share with my office mates. The stark contrast in our images was not lost on me and, after that uncomfortable elevator ride, I always carried my briefcase, even on nights when I had no intention of doing any work at home. Usually, I could fit my garden delights into the various briefcase pockets, thereby not depriving my coworkers while still appearing to be industrious.

Returning to the press conference, there was an air of excited anticipation as we began. The local TV stations were present, and the cameras were rolling. We managed to get through three-quarters of this press conference in a dignified manner. For me as emcee, however, there was just too much jumping up and down to introduce speakers. On my next-to-last trip to the podium, I began to rise from my seat, but never quite made it to my feet. Plunk! As I hit the floor, I had the presence of mind to make sure my skirt covered my knees and theatrically command, "Stop the cameras!" As people helped me to rise again, I wondered whether I was giving the Search Committee members or anyone else in the room the impression of leadership? When you suck it up quickly and without tears, does it demonstrate strength and resilience?

There is a short recuperation time after public falling. A person is expected to bounce back quicker than Silly Putty being slapped against a hard wall when what they really want to do is just sit and cry and allow their stomach, now residing just under the sinus cavities, to return to its normal position. That day at the press conference, I wanted to let someone else take over as emcee while the tremors in my voice and hands subsided and I slapped an ice pack on my hip.

Impossible. I needed to continue as if nothing out of the ordinary had happened. Why? Because I was representing not only myself but all people with disabilities. While public falling is borderline acceptable, public moaning and groaning and wallowing in self-pity is not. At stake was the image of all people with disabilities. It was my responsibility to counter the stereotype of a disabled person as weak and instead present a powerful persona. And, so, I did.

Airborne!

It was 1985 when I experienced the most humiliating event of my life, to that point. By this time, I had begun using a wheelchair for distances. Not walking meant I had more energy throughout the day. Further, I could make eye contact with my fellow humans rather than giving the appearance of searching for coins dropped on the ground. I never found any money, and if I had, would not have been able to pick it up anyway.

Unfortunately, I had not mastered the art of paying full attention to my surroundings while using the wheelchair. While exiting a restaurant with a colleague, I was so busy talking that I failed to notice a two-inch lip at the entrance. The footrests on my wheelchair jammed against the concrete and I promptly flew out of my chair and bounced onto the sidewalk.

This rapid-fire ejection occurred in the heavily trafficked State Circle in downtown Annapolis and was witnessed by countless drivers of slow-moving vehicles in search of a rare parking space. My friend, after determining that I was not hurt, began helping me to get back up into my chair. We both marveled that I had not even gotten a run in my pantyhose; after all, it is important to keep matters like this in perspective.

Later that evening, I relayed the whole story to my husband who, attempting to be empathetic, told me of the time he was with a mutual friend, a crutch user, who literally fell on his face when an attacking elevator door knocked his crutch out from under him. Having spent thirty-five years as a crutch user, I rolled my eyes and informed my husband that this analogy was like comparing apples to broccoli. To a crutch user, going splat is a given, like paying taxes. Sooner or later, it happens, whether weekly, biweekly, monthly, or annually. A savvy wheelchair user, on the other hand, just doesn't take flight under ordinary, everyday circumstances.

A few days after this great fall, my friend relayed that another mutual friend had witnessed the embarrassing scene and wondered what we were doing. When the friend who was with me told him the degrading truth, he responded, "Gee, if I'd known that, I would have stopped to help. I thought you two were fooling around as usual."

Less than a week later, I had the audacity to show my face again in the same restaurant with another colleague. The owner looked at me warily, no doubt wondering if I was there to advise him

I was suing and appeared to be relieved when all I wanted was a spinach salad and glass of iced tea.

The moral of this story is that our failures and falls will not deter us from achieving our goals if we maintain a sense of humor, don't take ourselves too seriously, and view our setbacks as temporary. This tale of woe also demonstrates that people who know us, like us, and respect us may share the pain of our falls and failures, but they don't dwell on them, and neither should we.

16

And Then We Were Four

The decision to have children happened, though not without unresolved ambivalence on my part. I worried I would not be a good mother, knowing I had a complicated relationship with my own mother, and that I would not be able to attend to many baby and toddler physical needs. If I could somehow make it through the early years, I reasoned, I would be a decent mom. Jim assured me that he would share the load, and I never doubted him. He also made promises we could not afford, including that we would hire a live-in nanny . . . in our smallish, three-bedroom, two-bath rancher. Suffice it to say, Mary Poppins never made an appearance.

After one ectopic pregnancy that ended in life saving surgery, we were expecting in 1982. I remained fully ambulatory for the first six months, until my blood pressure spiked. My center of gravity changed somewhat, but I never fell. Anticipating that I would require a wheelchair at some point in the pregnancy, we had borrowed a used one from a friend. Immediately upon learning of the blood pressure problem, I started using the wheelchair for work and other excursions outside my home and within a week averted a potential crisis for my little fetus.

I was fortunate to know two moms with disabilities, each older and wiser, who served as mentors. They offered reassurance and answered my many questions. One of my concerns was how to move the baby from one place to another since I did not want to risk falling while carrying him and had no intention of continuing to use the wheelchair after he was born. Baby wheels, of course, was the answer! Since we could not afford both a pram and a stroller, we purchased a reclining stroller, and I put Matthew into it whenever I needed to move him from one room to another.

Working at the DD Council meant I had access to information not yet available to the general public. One day a fabulous new publication came across my desk entitled *No More Stares*. It was full of photos of people with mobility disabilities going about their daily lives. One photo showed a mother in a wheelchair diapering her baby on a changing table that was wheelchair accessible. I showed this picture to Jim, my live-in handyman, and he built one for me prior to Matthew's arrival. Voilà, we were ready!

Matthew was born via scheduled C-section in early September that year. My obstetrician selected the anesthesiologist, who called me on a Saturday afternoon a few weeks before my delivery. He already had done some research on polio and scoliosis, and we discussed my situation and preferences. He appreciated my desire to be awake during the birth and agreed to try the spinal injection a half dozen times. I agreed to having general anesthesia if he could not succeed with the epidural. Speaking to this doctor in advance, then having him greet me when I entered the delivery room gave me confidence. He was successful with the epidural on the fifth try, and I was awake to witness my son's birth.

Matthew was an easy baby once we got beyond the breastfeeding experiment. My failure with it had nothing to do with my disability, and perhaps I gave up too soon. My son's well-being depended on adequate nutrition, though, and I was relieved with my decision to stop breastfeeding after just two months.

My father's final hospitalization occurred when Matthew was just two months old. It was expected given his late-stage cancer diagnosis. Jim and I packed the baby paraphernalia, fastened Matthew into his baby seat, and drove to Pittsburgh. Dad was absolutely thrilled to meet his grandson! The scene in the hospital room was both a joyful hello and tearful farewell. A week later we returned for my father's funeral.

Shortly before Matthew's birth, I turned thirty-five. Having been an only child myself, I wanted him to have a sibling. Time was of the essence. Two years later, we were pregnant again. This time I did not make it to the scheduled delivery date. Rebecca arrived six weeks early and shortly after midnight. Because this was an unscheduled delivery, the wonderful anesthesiologist was not on duty and the doctor who was there could not do the epidural injection successfully.

Unfortunately, I was not awake for Becca's birth. My tiny baby girl weighing under five pounds was healthy but needed to spend eleven days in the Neonatal Intensive Care Unit with a gavage tube through her nose for feeding purposes. Going home without her was lonely and stressful, although being spared the two a.m. feedings afforded me uninterrupted sleep and hastened my recovery.

A friend loaned me her pram, assuring greater comfort for my precious baby when I was moving her from room to room. Becca could sleep peacefully in the pram and enjoyed uninterrupted naps without having to be transferred into her crib. I was on maternity leave at work but was involved with a commission rewriting the law for the state's service delivery agency for people with developmental disabilities.

Baby Becca went along for the rides and meetings in Annapolis. At six weeks of age, she was still only the size of an average newborn. I carried her in a Snugli on my chest and used my wheelchair to go between my car and the building where the meetings were held. Another member of the commission referred to Becca as my "little mouse" and presented me with small porcelain animals for her at each meeting.

It was about this time that Becca developed colic, and our lives went from difficult to nearly impossible for a few months until it disappeared. Every night she would cry inconsolably for about three hours. We held, we rocked, we bounced, we rubbed her tummy, we positioned her in various ways, but nothing seemed to relieve her distress, and every night was the same. Evenings after work were unpleasant to say the least, but we somehow survived.

When she was three and a half months old, I was involved with an interagency conference for women with disabilities held over a weekend. As I drove to the hotel to deliver remarks on a Sunday morning, sans children, I thought that finally, at age thirty-seven, I was in way over my head. Whatever made me think I could manage parenting two children under the age of three? Now that I was in this situation, what should I do? I had secured my dream job as Executive Director of the DD Council, an outstanding career opportunity. Should I give it up and be a stay-at-home mother? We really needed my income, and being a full-time mother of an infant and toddler was not something I could do without help. Daytime assistance was an essential disability accommodation whether or not I was employed outside the home. Therefore, my continued income production was essential.

We persevered. Jim never complained. Heaven knows I did enough grousing for both of us. Becca outgrew the colic. Matthew hit a rough spot when his daycare provider terminated him abruptly for biting another child. Alhough this was typical behavior for a two-year-old, she had accepted additional children and was a bit overwhelmed. Luckily, we found a woman who would come into our home daily to care for both of our children. She was kind and an excellent care provider for Becca but not as comfortable with an active two-year-old boy. Proving that children are indeed resilient, Matthew endured this arrangement for a year and, when he was three, entered the marvelous Downtown Baltimore Child Care Center, where a rabbit hopped about freely and children were encouraged to explore their interests. He thrived in this program that stimulated his mind and cultivated his creativity. An additional benefit was the quality time he spent with either Jim or me during our commutes to and from Baltimore.

What a thrill to hold my first born, Matthew, in 1982.

Daughter Becca arrived in 1984, and we became a family of four.

No One Ever Patted My Tummy (Thankfully)

In my lifelong quest to prove that people with disabilities are not much different from people who have been spared this opportunity, I became pregnant. Actually, this was only a minor factor in my decision to have children, with the major one being a) curiosity—I wanted to explore another aspect of my womanhood; and b) the desire to fulfill my husband's strong maternal, yes maternal, instincts. This is not to say I had no maternal longings, just that I wasn't convinced I could successfully manage my own life, much less raise a child.

Reactions to this blatant exhibition of my womanhood were interesting. On the surface, friends appeared to be happy and supportive. Family reactions were fascinating. My mother, who had treated me as a typical child and teenager, was convinced I would be on bedrest for nine months. Aunt Margaret, known for her opinions on everything from bunions to bullfinches, was speechless for at least two minutes, then became so flustered she had to get off the phone.

Acquaintances were another matter. One of these, a man whose office was on the same floor as mine, approached me in the lobby at work after I had returned from maternity leave. By this time, I was walking again after having used a wheelchair during the final two months of pregnancy. He commented on how pleased he was to see me on foot once more. He went on to express his concern that my use of the wheelchair may have indicated a deteriorating condition. Had I known in advance how the man would react and considered that he was in heart attack age range, I might not have blurted out that I'd given birth to a darling baby boy three months earlier. *Dumbstruck* is the only word to describe his reaction. His eyes widened, his mouth dropped open, and he took a step backward. He could not have been more aghast had I ripped off a human face mask to reveal myself as an alien. Upon recovering his composure, he was exceedingly happy for me and, afterward, frequently stopped by my office to inquire about the baby and see the latest photos.

Another person, a woman, asked one of my coworkers about my health. She assumed that I was putting on weight due to a change in medication for my "condition," disability, that is, not pregnancy.

Strangers, a la the shopping mall variety, would sneak quick glances at me out of the corners of their eyes. A woman with a protruding belly exiting a maternity store is definitely a mother-to-be unless, of course, she's riding in a wheelchair. "They don't do that sort of thing, do they, Henry?" And my poor husband. Once these strangers decided that I was indeed with child, they would look at Jim as if he were an animal!

It wasn't until the end of my second pregnancy that I realized how this group of strangers had cheated me out of one of the most common experiences of pregnancy. About two weeks prior to delivery, a pregnant friend and I were commiserating about our uncomfortable circumstances. In exasperation she said, "And if one more stranger pats my abdomen, I'm going to scream!" Crestfallen at first, I recovered quickly and advised her to get a wheelchair or crutches, because through two pregnancies, no one ever patted my tummy.

17

An Interval as a Stay-At-Home Mom

With regrets and a few tears, I left the DD Council position midway through 1989. Jim had accepted a position as the General Counsel for the US Access Board, a fabulous opportunity, in Washington, DC. I was experiencing additional demands on my time due to having moved my mother several months earlier from Pittsburgh to a nursing facility about five miles from my home. A series of mini-strokes had seriously affected her ability to function independently. Suddenly I was a member of the "sandwich generation" wedged between the needs of young children and an aging parent. Something had to change, and I decided to leave the workforce and start a small consulting business where I could work from home and spend more time with my children and my mother.

My consulting business took off immediately, and for the next six years, I was able to accept as much work as I wanted and could sync it with my kids' schedules. During this six-year period, I really got into "mothering."

Volunteering in the kids' classrooms and at other school activities, taking my darlings out for lunch, driving them to and from soccer practice and dance classes, and hosting their neighborhood friends who came to play and often stayed for lunch meant my discretionary time was jampacked during the school year. I cooked, cleaned, crocheted, read for pleasure, and engaged in interesting work projects. Summers were mostly work-free and spent transporting the kids to day camps and taking them to the neighbor's pool and to various activities. During this time in my life, I began to reflect upon my experiences as a person with a disability and wrote most of the essays contained herein.

The doorbell rang one morning while I was busily researching grants for a client. It was my neighbor, Mark Houck, who handed me a large brown envelope and said, "You and Jim are invited to Margaret Ann's birthday party." He went on to explain that the party for his wife was a murder mystery event where each guest would assume the role assigned, and the details were in the envelope. The party was to be held at a bed and breakfast inn not too far away. Happy for the role of a diva, not the corpse, I wore oversized, dangling earrings and a few oxther fashionable items. In retrospect, I would have made a great victim given my expertise at falling. This fun and memorable night cemented the friendships with neighbors and with Margaret Ann's large family. Although Jim and I moved from that wonderful neighborhood eighteen years ago to a more accessible home, we remain close friends and socialize often with our former neighbors.

The pinochle group began in 1995. Initiated by another neighbor, Karen Trennepohl, the mainstays have been neighbors from Tyler Drive and the East Side gang from Baltimore County. This latter group was led by Margaret Ann's late father Jack Nolan, a charismatic, life of the party person. Laughs abound when this less than serious group gathers monthly.

One of my great summer joys was sharing my interest in baseball with my son. Long ago in the era of Roberto Clemente and Willie Mays, I cultivated my own interest in baseball in order to bond with my father, who loved that sport. During my stay-at-home mom time, I had the luxury of taking Matthew to baseball games on summer weeknights since I didn't need to get up at the crack of dawn and rush to work. My sports bond with Matthew continues to this day with frequent phone calls that include discussions about football or baseball.

Wednesday evenings and Sundays were devoted to my mother. Each Sunday, either Jim or I drove her to our home before lunch and she stayed through dinner. I believe these outings and being involved with her grandchildren to the extent that she could, were what kept her alive for four years living in a nursing facility.

Although my life was rich and full during this six-year hiatus from the workforce, I missed the constant interaction with my colleagues and being on top of the latest happenings in the disability field. At a time prior to the internet, regular phone or in-person contact with colleagues to keep abreast of new developments was essential. I interacted with some colleagues through my consulting work, yet it was not enough. As time passed, I also worried that I would not be able to re-enter the workforce at the same level as when I left. My worries increased when I applied and was not hired for two executive director jobs. The rejections happened within the same week, leaving me temporarily devastated.

As I reflect on those rejections and my six years as a stay-at-home mom, I realize my timing to re-enter the workforce was premature. Although my identity as an adult was closely connected to my work, I cherish the memories of those six years when work was adjusted to meet the needs of my family. My investment of time with my children was priceless and continues to pay off in their adult lives and in our closeness as a family.

What's a mother to do when her girl needs to see Mickey and Minnie at Disney World?

Spunky

"You sure are spunky," he said. At first, it seemed like one of those well-intended, but often peculiar, remarks made by a stranger without a disability. After further reflection, I am comfortable with this statement and consider it the highest compliment and one I have earned.

It happened on a day trip to Philadelphia where we had gone as a family to check out a swim spa that we were considering buying. I deliberately used the term "check out" because we were not merely looking at this fabulous piece of equipment, we came prepared to get fully immersed. We brought swimsuits, towels, a trusty hair dryer, and a curling iron. Heaven forbid that I might be in an accident on the way home with unruly hair!

The demo swim spa was located at the rear of a warehouse where the spas were built and prepared for shipping. We left the chilly warehouse and entered a nicely appointed and warm room complete with a shower and changing area.

My kids, ages nine and eleven at the time, went bonkers when they saw the spa and proceeded to set a new world record for stripping off their clothes. At last, I understood why they were so intent on wearing their swimsuits under their clothes, despite my telling them there was a changing room. I realized when I saw the excited looks in their eyes that I had made a major mothering faux pas. I had not considered the impact that five fall and winter months without swimming could have on kids this age. I had forgotten to review the code of appropriate conduct for this occasion and setting—too late—they had hopped in.

Approaching the chaos as any responsible mother would, I retreated to the changing room and left my husband to deal with the young ones. He was in deep conversation with our host, one of the company owners, discussing the specifications, warranties, etc. for the swim spa. He volunteered later that evening that he thought the children had been exceptionally well behaved. Ignorance really is bliss.

Wearing my swimsuit in front of the swim spa dealer in a twenty-by-twenty-foot space on a Saturday in January when not a trace of a tan remains was the most daunting aspect of this trip. I entered the water as hastily as my crippled body could manage without making eye contact with our host until I was immersed up to my neck—tricky since the spa was only three feet deep. Water may be transparent, but at least it covers better than air, especially when it's stirred up.

By this time, my darlings were really churning it, and I tried in earnest to settle them. They finally did calm down—a bit—though not before splashing and soaking our host, who was still dressed in street clothes. Time to avoid eye contact again.

It was as I emerged from my swim that our host uttered the "spunky" remark. Having been described many times as courageous, of course, I assumed this was a disability-related comment. It occurred to me later, though, that he might have meant it in relationship to my unruly children, as in "You've got to be mighty spunky to parent those two." He did not, however, tell my husband, the other parent of "those two," that he was spunky. The comment might also have been related to my having enough nerve to don a swimsuit. You know, spunky, as in rhymes with chunky.

Whatever the intent, the more I think about the word "spunky," the more I like it. *Spunky* is a great descriptor. It implies strength and energy with a generous dose of humor. It is a word that describes our pioneer forefathers and mothers and athletes who bounce back. It acknowledges people who live life to the fullest and play the hand they're dealt without complaint.

I remember wanting a nickname in high school. Finally, I have one—Spunky. I once filled out a job application that asked for any nicknames. Entering

Spunky might have corrected any misperceptions about slowing down due to the combined effects of disability and age. Probably not, though, and opting for professionalism is always a safe and better choice when job seeking.

Yes, we bought an Endless Pool which I use daily for exercise. It was also a great scene for our 1994 Christmas card.

A Night in Left Field

I sat in left field for the first time. Right field? Yes, I had grown up on baseball in right field in Pittsburgh, watching the late, great Roberto Clemente foil the scoring aspirations of unsuspecting baserunners with his jaw dropping throws. Left field was an altogether different story. How would I feel being in "left field"? The phrase alone evokes images of lost souls searching for answers to cosmic questions. I need not fear. Left field at Camden Yards may have contained a few lost souls, but they were most likely refugees from Section 70 in search of seats that wouldn't land them in a chiropractor's office.

My migration to left field was caused by my son's growing interest in baseball and its potential impact on the family's recreation budget. It's hard to explain to a ten-year-old why we could only go to one baseball game each season when his friends' parents could get free tickets through work to attend several. Why didn't my husband or I work for a business that owned a sky box? Good question. Because we preferred to subsist at the public trough? It was an easier answer than trying to explain being inspired by President Kennedy's stirring call to public service many years ago.

I took some drastic measures to please my son. First, I removed my husband from the guest list. He, who was once a soda vendor at Shea Stadium, really did not appreciate baseball and preferred to wander around the concourse, sort of open-air window shopping until the third inning when he began "suggesting" that we go home. Next to be uninvited was my daughter whose main interest at age eight seemed to be cotton candy. These actions meant we could double the number of games we could attend. Then we ditched the box seats and moved to the back of the stadium, i.e., left field where seats could be purchased at half the price. Granted, these seats were much farther from the action than we were accustomed to, and we had to invest in binoculars. Although my husband's left eyebrow jerked up when he saw the binocular purchase on the VISA receipt, I was quick to point out that good binoculars could last a lifetime. Note to self: do not misplace the binoculars.

The night of our first excursion in left field arrived about a month after sitting through a boring game in the lower boxes some fifteen rows behind home plate watching the 1993 Blue Jays demonstrate why a dozen of them should be chosen for the All-Star game. It was the eighth inning that night before I realized the "holes" (rhymes with poles) the young guys in front of us kept talking about was really Orioles catcher Chris Hoiles (rhymes with boils) and not sloppy defensive play. Ahhh, a classic example of the Baltimore accent, Hon!

The evening of our first game in left field got off to a rocky start when the gate attendant opened my son's tote bag in search of something illegal and inadvertently dumped the container of my tossed salad. Seeing the shredded carrots and wilted lettuce laying pathetically in my son's well-worn baseball glove was a good excuse to abandon healthy eating for the evening and scarf down a hot dog.

Overall, it was a good game although it bogged down for several innings as baseball games are inclined to do. The left field entertainment began during this big lull. Fans in front of us launched a big beach ball high into the air, keeping it narrowly out of reach of the ushers. It was confiscated finally, but nearly every inning a group would start tossing a large balloon until those too were grabbed by the ushers. These fans came prepared.

Somewhere around the seventh inning, the Orioles began to score, but the action was thwarted by a series of pitching changes. It was then that a group of inebriated men jumped on top of their seats and began dancing, singing and howling at the full moon suspended in picture perfect form over the adjacent warehouse. Interestingly, the ushers did not escort the men from the stadium, though they were far more distracting than the beach ball and balloons. I rarely imbibe in alcohol and don't condone its abuse, but these men kept it clean, put on a good show and involved everyone in the surrounding seats. My son and I agreed it was the best game we had ever attended (and the Orioles won!), because it was so participatory. On our way home we worried about whether the men would return safely to their homes, prompting one of those values laden conversations about drinking and driving that all parents love. Happily, we saw the men a few weeks later when we sat in left field again. They were more subdued this time. Alas, no full moon.

The summer of '93 was a special time for my son and me. It was a time when I did not have the pressures of a full-time demanding job. It was a time when I could enjoy my son's excitement at having a chance to catch a ball or wait in line after a game to collect a player's autograph. Most importantly, it was a time of bonding between us that, hopefully, will never be forgotten or destroyed. And much of it happened that night and several others in left field.

18

People on the Go

Shortly after I left the Maryland Developmental Disabilities Council, Cristy Marchand called asking me to undertake a project. Upon arriving in Maryland a few months earlier as the new Executive Director of The Arc Maryland, Cristy was disappointed by the lack of a robust self-advocacy movement among people with intellectual disabilities. She wanted to ignite one, thereby giving The Arc's Board of Directors and the local chapters ongoing input from the grassroots. As a believer in self-advocacy, I enthusiastically agreed, and this became my first contract as a consultant.

One problem. I discovered immediately that facilitating a group of people who had little, if any, experience with meetings required a different skill set than being the policy wonk, grant maker, and systems change agent I had become at the DD Council.

At the group's first meeting, I asked two questions: 1) what is going right or well in your life; and 2) what is not going well? The approximately twenty-five people at the meeting identified four, count 'em—1, 2, 3, 4—things that were going well in their lives. Yet they filled four poster-size pages with "what was not going well." Their recurring theme was that "people ask us what we want or don't want, but nothing ever changes." Good theme. We could build one or more projects around this theme. By the end of the meeting, however, the group had become distracted and decided their first endeavor would be a fundraiser—a car wash.

Staging a car wash was not what I expected when I signed on for this job. Here I was, over forty, a wife, mother, and former Executive Director of a highly visible state agency suddenly organizing a car wash. My new role was to empower, not question the groups' decisions, though, so I bought a jug of detergent at the Goodyear Tire Store, gathered some old towels, called a few people without disabilities to help, and traveled down the road to Wheaton for this big event.

The day dawned with a crystal blue sky, beautiful sunshine, and temperatures hovering in the mid-seventies. The Montgomery County contingent had arranged to hold the car wash at a local fire station. Local Arc chapters transported the group members from around the state. Group members from the closest counties arrived first and set to work, putting up a sign and washing cars of the first customers. I stationed myself beside a woman who had a recent hip replacement to get her started with collecting the money. Once satisfied that she could make change and protect the money, I moved about offering tips. I knew nothing about car washes, but giving advice is what a consultant does, right? By 11:30 a.m., the large group from north of Baltimore had not arrived. The early arrivals were tiring rapidly. I worried about not having recruited enough allies to help with this endeavor. Suddenly, the van pulled in with the Harford County group—relief for the early washers had arrived. Not so fast. The Harford group had been on their van over two hours and made a beeline to a picnic table in the shade for lunch. Priorities.

To their credit, the late arrivals ate quickly and brought an abundance of new energy to the event, as did Cristy, who arrived around the same time. Afternoon business was plentiful, and the group made over $300 for the day. The most memorable customer came around two p.m., when there was a waiting line. He was dressed in a three-piece navy pinstriped suit with wingtip shoes. Undeterred by having to wait in line, yet still in a bit of a hurry, he jumped out to help the self-advocates wash his car. If he got splashed while rinsing his car, he never complained and hopped back in with a wave and a big smile as he drove away.

At three p.m., I heard a loud chorus groan and exclaim, "Oh, no!" I turned and laughed to see the fire fighters pulling out the big hook-and-ladder truck to be washed. All hands were needed for this job, and they thoroughly enjoyed the challenge it presented.

The self-advocacy group picked a name at their third meeting, and they could not have chosen a more appropriate one. They became People on the Go (POG), a high energy name for a group with big ambitions.

About a year into their quarterly meetings, the group hosted a guest speaker, Kathleen Wolf, then Deputy Director of the Maryland Developmental Disabilities Administration, the main funding source of supports and services for people with intellectual and developmental disabilities. Kathee presented a draft of "The People Plan" developed by DDA that was designed to focus attention on important benchmarks to assure quality and person-centeredness. At the conclusion of her presentation, Kathee invited the group to contribute their ideas. Group members were excited but unsure about next steps. They turned to me asking, "What can we do?"

At that point, "The People Plan" had basic concepts, such as "people have privacy" and "people participate in the community." I began by asking the group, how would I know if you participate in the community? I could ask you, but what if you could not answer my question? What signs should I look for to know if a person participates in their community? Thus began the second People on the Go project known as "The Signs of Quality." I visited each member of the group at their home or day program gathering their ideas. Upon reading my summary, Cristy decided to capture the group's great thoughts in a publication. When that was completed, she called asking me to recommend a member of the group to serve as the keynote speaker at The Arc's upcoming annual conference. At that point in time, no one in the group had any public-speaking experience.

Rather than choose only one keynoter, I selected a panel of ten representatives from around the state. The panel was arranged in a horseshoe formation, allowing them to see each other. I sat in the first row of the audience and asked them the same questions as I had done when I visited them at home. We gathered in my hotel room the evening prior to their presentation and rehearsed. The People on the Go keynote was well received and led to members of the group receiving more speaking invitations.

Approximately a year after the ADA became law, the Disability Rights Education and Defense Fund based in California, received a federal contract to conduct training for people with disabilities on the law and how to use it. The training was similar to the PILCOP training on Section 504 that I had attended in 1977. Cristy asked me to select, accompany, and mentor two of the POG members at this training. Debbie, Rebecca, and I went to DC for the three-day training. Although the subject matter was new to both women and difficult for them to understand, participating in this training was a confidence-booster.

I sat between the two women in the small breakout session. At the end of the first small group meeting, the man sitting on the other side of Debbie asked her if she would help put his materials in the backpack on his wheelchair. Her face lit up and she eagerly jumped up to help him, then faithfully assisted him with retrieving and repacking his materials at each small group session. A friendship was forming and one of my mentees was feeling included and valued.

The three of us were joined at lunch by Dave, one of the trainees from Pittsburgh. Dave became our regular fourth at meals and breaktime. When Debbie and Rebecca received their small group assignments, i.e., to explain a key concept of the ADA, Dave assisted with my mentoring of the two POG members.

Before taking her seat at the plenary session on the third morning, Rebecca was glowing and said to me, "People here like me." Blinking away some tears, I replied, "Of course they do; you're a really nice person." This wonderful woman was full of self-doubts and had not experienced the opportunity to make new friends that so many of us enjoy when we attend trainings or conferences.

In the end, Debbie and Rebecca were so popular with the other participants, they both were invited to join groups on the last night for dinner. I had done my job and happily faded into the background for an evening of relaxation prior to heading home to my lively household.

Two of the driving concerns of POG were the use of the "R" word and eliminating institutions. Although I did not like the "R" word, I thought at one point the term *mental retardation* could become a source of disability pride for people with that label. My basis of comparison was the growing source of pride those of us with physical disabilities were experiencing as the disability rights movement took hold. However, the term *mental retardation* had become more than a diagnosis or condition. Thanks to Cristy's wisdom and the pain expressed by the POG members, I came to view the "R" word as a pejorative term that needed to be eliminated. Members of our group and people with intellectual disabilities across the country expressed their disdain for the "R" word, and the Board of Directors of The

Association for Retarded Citizens changed its name to The Arc and all local chapters did the same.

Closing institutions was a more difficult matter requiring years of advocacy. People on the Go focused on the Great Oaks Center located near the Washington Beltway. They spoke out and wrote letters. They were joined in opposition by The Arc Maryland and aided by a lawsuit filed by the Maryland Disability Law Center in support of moving all residents to community-based programs. Finally, in 1996 it closed.

Serving as facilitator of People on the Go for five years is an experience I will never forget. We had fun, and I have delightful memories indelibly etched in my mind. At the outset, I felt ill-equipped to assist the group, and after each meeting would share my frustrations with my husband. Thanks to his encouragement, I continued. The group members learned how to participate in meetings, and I learned patience and strategies for drawing out their talents and ideas. Most importantly, I learned that holding a fundraiser, i.e., the car wash, was tremendously empowering. Choosing to hold it when the group was just beginning was a stroke of genius on their part. Yes, indeed, the members of People on the Go were great teachers!

The Signs of Quality project described above culminated with five members of the group presenting the keynote and a workshop at a family support conference in San Antonio attended by more than 500 people. Traveling to and from San Antonio with this group and sharing a room with one of the women was an enjoyable experience and my final one prior to leaving them before opening Independence Now.

I am proud of the growth of group members during my time with them. In our final two-plus years, someone announced a new job or a move to their own apartment or condo at every meeting. They truly were People on the Go!

The self-advocacy group People on the Go is still together in 2023. It now has a paid policy director, and many of the original members continue to participate.

19

A Nonprofit Entrepreneur

One day while minding my consulting business, I received a call from Joanna Clarke, who was, at the time, Director of the Disability Resources Division in Montgomery County, Maryland's most populated jurisdiction. "Funding will soon be available to start a new Center for Independent Living in Maryland," she announced, "and the state's priority is the DC suburban counties. "Would you be willing to write the grant to bring that funding to our area?" she continued. "And, oh, by the way, I hear you do some pro bono work," Joanna added. Laughingly, I agreed.

I had long admired the independent living movement from afar. Its underlying philosophy resonates with me. Simply stated, that philosophy is: a) the person with the disability knows best and should be making all decisions about their lives and b) our problems are largely created by inaccessible environments and either negative or paternalistic attitudes toward disability.

Joanna invited her counterpart in Prince George's County, Bea Rodgers, to become a partner in this venture, and Bea became the third musketeer. These two well-known leaders in their respective counties asked a few members of their advisory commissions to a meeting with me. I facilitated a discussion about the needs among people with various disabilities in the two counties. The participants' insights became the priorities within the grant application. Moral support from Joanna and Bea was valuable and appreciated as I prepared the application.

The first task at hand was to incorporate this new nonprofit. The late disability activist Bill Lee; Marsha Mazz, who had previously worked at the center for independent living in Northern Virginia; and Maggie Roffee, who worked at the former President's Committee on People with Disabilities, joined me as the four necessary incorporators. For the next few months, I prepared and filed the Articles of Incorporation, wrote a winning grant application, and recruited additional members for the board of directors. Pat Laird was one of the original board members who eventually became the longest-serving volunteer on the board. Every board needs a financial expert and Kathleen Wolf, formerly Deputy Director of the Developmental Disabilities Administration, stepped up to fill the Treasurer's role.

Once we were notified of funding, I needed to choose whether to become the full-time Executive Director of the new organization, named Independence Now (IN), or continue with my consulting business and allow the board of directors to hire someone else. Recognizing the insufficiency of the funding obtained through the federal grant and believing in my ability to raise funding and stabilize this highly vulnerable organization, I rolled up my sleeves and signed on for the job. From fall 1994 through winter 1995, I developed the organizational structure, submitted the applications for 501(c)(3) status and state sales tax exemption, secured our EIN, drafted policies and procedures for board approval, found office space, and hired staff.

Because we had only a small amount of public funding, the dilemma I faced was whether to pay myself and an assistant or hire staff to provide services and advocacy. I chose to forego a salary for the first year of the organization's operation and hired three staff. "Good," said IN's first board chairman, Bill Lee, "I was worried we wouldn't be able to offer any services." For better or worse, I was suddenly a nonprofit entrepreneur. This new organization named Independence Now opened in April 1995 and within a year had sufficient funding for me to be added to the payroll.

My extensive network of connections built over many years proved to be a bonanza. I will be forever grateful to those who made both large and modest donations to IN during those early years and to my clever, dedicated board members who creatively thought of ways to generate funding.

I spent twelve years as the Executive Director, stabilizing and growing the organization. Independence Now continues to thrive nearly thirty years later and has employed numerous people with various disabilities over the course of its existence.

Hiring people with disabilities, many of whom had been unsuccessful in their job searches and underestimated by other employers, was gratifying. The stories of employment rejection poured out during interviews where my last question was, "Tell me about your job search. Have you experienced any employment discrimination?" My guess is that I could ask that question of applicants with disabilities today and still hear similar answers.

If there is a single action that could reduce employment discrimination against people with disabilities, it would be for all employers to provide training and/or technical assistance for their staff who conduct interviews so they understand how to draw out the best in all applicants. Interviewers inevitably will meet candidates with invisible disabilities who have difficulty with eye contact, experience anxiety, or have a spotty employment history. Some of these individuals will have the skills and motivation to succeed on the job but may require an interviewer with an open mind who can see their potential and who has the vision of how to immerse them in the company culture. Hiring managers should refrain from imagining themselves doing the job if they were blind, for instance, and instead ask the applicant to explain how they would perform "essential functions" of the job.

20

INnovation at IN

We did some groundbreaking and exciting work while I was at Independence Now (IN). Because it was known that one of my consulting projects was a study of people leaving nursing facilities in two states through requirements of the Omnibus Budget Reconciliation Act of 1987, referrals of non-elderly people who wanted to leave nursing facilities began pouring in immediately. Within two weeks of our opening, one man who was living in a nursing facility about ten miles from our office burst through our door exclaiming, "I hear you can get me out of a nursing facility!" Given the distance he had to travel and the fact that he had no personal transportation and not much money, reaching our office was a remarkable feat. At one time, he had been an urban planner; hence, he was able and downright eager to take charge of locating wheelchair accessible and affordable community housing. All he needed was for our staff to provide him with the information he needed every step along the way.

While Executive Director at the Developmental Disabilities Council, I learned it is quicker to convince those working in bureaucracy to change their practices by showing them what can be done and producing desirable outcomes. I applied this knowledge at Independence Now, and we became the first organization in Maryland to assist people to move from nursing facilities to homes of their own in the community. Our successes converted the skeptics into believers.

It was a slow process, however, given the challenge of finding affordable and accessible housing and the very limited personal care programs in Maryland at the time. Our sister organization in the Baltimore area was inspired and replicated our nursing facility transition program.

After a few years, we were helped by the late Gayle Hafner, a persistent lawyer and visionary advocate with a disability, who lobbied the Maryland General Assembly to enact state legislation entitled Money Follows the Individual Accountability Act. Gayle was aware of what we were doing in Maryland on a shoestring and what was happening in other states. This new law she drafted and steered through the General Assembly enabled Maryland to obtain federal grants to expand and intensify the efforts for people of all ages throughout the state to receive home and community based services rather than living in nursing facilities. One of the federal grants enabled Independence Now to finally hire a Housing Director, James Freeny, who worked tirelessly to connect people with affordable and accessible rental housing.

Another opportunity creating statewide visibility for IN was our receipt of a grant from the Social Security Administration to provide information throughout Maryland on the Social Security Work Incentives. This project, directed by the talented and detail-oriented Tonya Gilchrist addressed the fears of people with disabilities about losing their SSI or SSDI income and the all-important health insurance through Medicare or Medicaid. Armed with an understanding of the work incentives, many Marylanders chose employment.

I joined with other employment advocates to form a group dedicated to helping Maryland create a Medicaid Buy-In Program that would enable people who worked to pay a monthly premium to Medicaid for health insurance. Since no other health insurer covers long-term care, people who required in-home assistance with their personal care were eager for a buy-in opportunity. We met monthly for more than a year before we crafted legislation for this purpose. The legislation had significant support in the General Assembly and finally began enrolling people in 2006.

21

Happy Hours in Nursing Homes?

Like most Americans, I had considerable anxiety following the September 11, 2001 attacks on our country. To cope, I looked at the MSN homepage periodically at work to see if there were new developments. One day while browsing, I noticed a headline about a nursing home in Ireland that had added a pub and immediately clicked on it. The Irish facility invited and welcomed the community to join their residents at the pub. New opportunities for socialization and friendships enhanced the lives of both groups.

I pondered this powerful news article overnight. At the time, there were fifty-two nursing facilities in the two counties served by Independence Now. Convincing even one of them to add a pub would be a gargantuan task. We could, however, do "happy hours" at the facilities where there was a significant population of non-elderly residents.

The happy hours would be fun with snacks, non-alcoholic beverages, crafts, games, and information about housing and community living services. Yes, happy hour outreach to people stuck in nursing facilities who would like to rebuild their lives could be a winning strategy!

I excitedly shared the idea with our Director of Independent Living Services, Lorraine Nawara. Lorraine had an abundance of energy and was possibly the most organized person I had ever met. She was "all in" and led our happy hours, making the arrangements and engaging our staff. These outreach events were a huge success and evolved over time. One of my friends donated a karaoke machine, adding to our enjoyment. Lorraine found a dance instructor who specialized in teaching wheelchair users how to give it a whirl.

Those who participated in our happy hours had fun and met our staff who would assist them to complete the lengthy applications for housing vouchers or subsidized housing. Staff also assisted them to apply for funding for personal care, assistive technology, durable medical equipment, and all other items or services they needed. One by one, people moved out of institutions and into their own homes. No one ever expressed the desire to return to institutional living.

22

Youth Is Definitely Not Wasted on the Young!

Another pioneering effort by Independence Now was to replicate the California Youth Leadership Forum, a weeklong program for high school students with all disabilities held each summer on a college campus. The program was a creation of the California Governor's Committee on Employment of People with Disabilities. One of IN's board members, Maggie Roffee, who worked at what was then called the President's Committee on Employment of People with Disabilities, volunteered at the California program one summer. Maggie was suitably impressed and, upon her return to Washington, secured funding for replication training of the California program. When no one from the Maryland Governor's Committee on Employment was able to attend the training, Maggie asked me to go. I packed my suitcase and got an emergency eleventh hour myringotomy for an ear infection before flying to Sacramento.

Upon returning I shared my excitement about the YLF (Youth Leadership Forum) with Bea Rodgers, who by that time was Director of the Governor's Office for Individuals with Disabilities (it later became the Department of Disabilities) and Dr. Nancy Grasmick, State Superintendent of Schools. Both contributed financial and personnel support from their respective agencies, essential for the success of the MD-YLF (Maryland Youth Leadership Forum).

Planning for the MD-YLF commenced shortly after meeting with Bea and Nancy. The staff who they committed were top notch and excited about the program. Jade Gingerich, Amy Pleet, Berenda Riedl, and Lee Murphy comprised the original Steering Committee. We held meetings at my office, and everyone had a role from recruiting volunteer staff for the week-long activities to reaching out to all local school systems to find students interested in attending this new program with no track record.

Finally, we launched the program at Bowie State University in July 2000. By now, I was in my fifties, yet found myself shopping for extra-long sheets for my week-long stay in a college dorm. As staff, we checked in the day before the students arrived and conducted our training. We were settled, but all of us were nervous. What if this program was a total bust?

A cute redheaded teen zipped past me in her wheelchair as I entered the dorm to welcome the students and their parents who were dropping them off. I said hello to her, and she ignored me. This was Jessica, and, immediately, I pegged her as the student most like me when I was her age. She had that air of faux confidence.

The first year of the MD-YLF was an enormous success. Many of the students who attended that year returned in future years as volunteers. Some alumni continue to stay in touch with one or more of us. When I had finally raised enough money to pay for a YLF Coordinator, I hired Jessica, who by then had graduated from the University of Maryland.

My affinity for the YLF stemmed from my own experiences as a teen with a disability. It was the most difficult period of my life, marked by self-imposed estrangement from my peer group and the resulting loneliness. I recall longing to read books written by an adult with a physical disability who had navigated his or her teen years successfully, but I could not find one. A summer leadership program would have been just the ticket since it is loaded with adult speakers who experience disabilities. The MD-YLF was my gift to teens with disabilities and I have never for a moment regretted the countless hours I devoted to organizing it.

23

If My Parents Could See Me Now

Twelve years of stabilizing and growing Independence Now took its toll. Exhausted and at least temporarily out of new ideas, I needed a sabbatical but instead gave my board of directors twelve months' notice to search for my replacement. Though I was preparing to leave, I had not identified my next step when a new governor was elected. Suddenly, there was an opportunity of great interest.

Martin O'Malley was sworn in as Maryland's sixty-first governor in January 2007. Having served as Baltimore's mayor, he was widely regarded as a rising political star. Unfortunately, none of the disability advocates seemed to have a connection to him. I decided to take an early exit ramp from Independence Now and apply for a senior-level position, Secretary of the Department of Disabilities (MDOD), in his new administration. I gathered support from people the new governor trusted, and he appointed me to this cabinet-level position.

My cousin Tom Allen said it best in congratulating me on this new position: "Your parents would be so proud." When I was in high school, my dad once told me I should get some secretarial skills so that I wouldn't have to work in a sheltered workshop. While I never got those secretarial skills, i.e., typing and shorthand, I was now a secretary or rather, Madame Secretary. Yes, my parents would be proud.

Governor O'Malley appointed subject matter experts to lead his cabinet departments. My knowledge of disability policy and issues was complemented by the expertise of my fellow cabinet members in the areas of housing, child welfare and social services, health, juvenile services, public safety and corrections, and labor. Not surprisingly, each of these fellow cabinet members became collaborators on various projects, and it truly was a pleasure working with them.

Closing Rosewood

The most urgent disability matter facing Governor O'Malley presented itself immediately. Maryland's oldest state institution, Rosewood, had been the target of the advocacy community for many years. We all wanted it closed. There had been numerous citations by the Centers for Medicare and Medicaid Services dating back to the 1980s that documented the serious problems at this facility. Although the state had funded changes, conditions at Rosewood improved very little and recent media scrutiny had been plentiful and unflattering. I advised Governor O'Malley to close Rosewood. I lobbied the Secretary of the Department of Health and Mental Hygiene, John Colmers, under whose auspices the institution came, to close Rosewood. Although the governor appreciated my advice and understood the growing concerns that Rosewood was not a fit place for people to live, he nevertheless was concerned, and rightly so, about the families who were fearful of having their sons and daughters moved to community-based services. He wisely chose to meet with the families prior to holding a press conference to announce the closure and was touched by their stories. Following the governor's lead, Secretary Colmers oversaw a process of closing Rosewood that was respectful of the families and engaged them as much as they wanted to participate. Over the course of the next sixteen months, each family was assisted in selecting a community service provider and was supported during the transition from institution to community living. The last person left Rosewood on May 22, 2009, just sixteen months after the governor's announcement.

The Fitness and Athletics Bill

Before she was a renowned Paralympic champion, Tatyana McFadden was a teenage girl living in Howard County, MD who wanted to participate with her high school track team as a wheelchair racer. Her school system refused to permit this, citing safety concerns. Tatyana and her mother, Deborah McFadden, a former official in the administration of President George H.W. Bush, filed a lawsuit in 2005. They prevailed but also wanted to enshrine into law the right of all students with disabilities to engage in both physical education and sports in their schools.

We, at the Department of Disabilities, enthusiastically supported state legislation they conceived, assuring students with all disabilities had access to physical education and athletic competition in public schools across the state. In the summer of 2007, we convened meetings of organizations including Special Olympics and Disabled Sports USA, along with traditional disability advocates, in preparation for a Fitness and Athletics bill to be introduced and considered by the Maryland General Assembly in the 2008 Session. This large and unified push resulted in the bill's passage. Once Governor O'Malley signed the bill into law, we organized an enjoyable celebration with remarks and demonstrations by various disabled athletes.

Employment

Throughout my time as Secretary, my top priority was employment. The high unemployment rate among people with disabilities is the anchor that weighs them down and keeps them in poverty. Having a job and the income it produces is the ultimate method of empowerment. Thanks to the energy, creativity, and overall brilliance of Jade Gingerich, MDOD's Director of Employment Policy, we pushed the employment agenda with numerous initiatives. By promoting the Social Security Work Incentives, especially the Medicaid Buy-in, through numerous workshops held in concert with our Department of Labor, Licensing and Regulation, we were addressing the fear many people have of losing health insurance through Medicare. We attached ourselves to the anticipated creation of new jobs through the Base Realignment and Closure when the US Department of Defense transferred certain responsibilities from other states into Maryland. One important strategy for any cabinet agency is to connect its work to the governor's priorities. Governor O'Malley frequently said we have "No Spare Marylanders" when referring to creating new employment opportunities and making certain that our youth were fully prepared to enter the workforce. "No Spare Marylander" became our mantra, and we labeled items given out at our workshops, such as thumb drives, messenger bags, and small office-on-the-go kits with this message. We hoped that this frequent repetition would support people's belief that they could work despite having little job success in the past.

Housing

My knowledge of the vast number of Marylanders stuck in nursing facilities required action on housing. Our housing collaboration with the Harry and Jeanette Weinberg Foundation resulted in their $2 million investment to create affordable units within apartment complexes. It captured the attention of the US Department of Housing and Urban Development, and as a result, Maryland was awarded an additional $10 million for this purpose. The effort continues to produce beneficial results for Marylanders with disabilities who want to live in affordable and well-maintained rental units.

Early in my tenure as Secretary of the Department of Disabilities, I co-chaired a summer study group on "visitable housing" with the Secretary of Housing and Community Development. Visitable housing is defined as single-family or owner-occupied housing designed in such a way that it can be lived in or visited by people who have trouble with steps or who use wheelchairs or walkers. A house is visitable when it meets three basic requirements:

- one zero-step entrance;
- doors with thirty-two inches of clear passage space; and
- one bathroom on the main floor that you can use in a wheelchair.

The summer study group was formed by the Maryland General Assembly when the home builders group opposed a bill championed by disability advocates that would have required construction of new single-family housing to be visitable. During our deliberations, we heard repeated objections and rationale from the home builders about how visitable housing would add significantly to the cost and be impossible in various terrains.

I cringed more than a few times during this summer study group witnessing the intransigence of the home builders' representative and realizing that power rested with the industry, not the disability advocates. Unfortunately, nothing changed.

On Being Included

Most of my work over the years would not produce any personal benefit. Housing, however, is a personal issue. By 2000, I used a wheelchair most of the time. Thus, inaccessible housing means I cannot participate in my neighborhood book club or in other social gatherings at most people's homes.

I must say, though, that friends and allies do their best to include me. Our trusty portable ramp makes it possible for me to get into houses with three steps or less. We purchased the ramp after attending a fundraiser for a local autism group. Governor O'Malley had been invited to attend this event being held at a private home. He had another commitment and asked me to attend in his place. Since this home was in a community adjacent to where I lived, Jim and I did a drive-by to see if it would be possible for me to get into this house. When my assistant called to offer my regrets because I could not navigate the three steps, the homeowner announced she would rent a ramp. Honestly, I don't believe I had ever felt more valued and included. Everyone attending the fundraiser was pleased by my attendance and made me feel welcome. I was touched by this homeowner's kindness.

High Visibility

Serving in a governor's cabinet means having a platform for policy change, being on call 24/7, plus having an abundance of ceremonial duties. In seven years, I traversed the state, appearing at disability-related events and at the governor's town halls and Capitals for a Day. At the latter, the governor held a cabinet meeting in various localities around the state, declaring each as capital for the day. Following cabinet meetings, each Secretary met with our local counterparts to learn more about their issues and activities. Having no local counterparts, I visited many nonprofit disability organizations and learned more about their outstanding supports and services to people with various disabilities.

I was working at home one afternoon in the winter of 2013 when I had a call from Janice Jackson, whose friendship I cherish. Janice sustained a spinal cord injury after being struck by a car on the Washington Beltway many years before. With great excitement, Janice said, "You're not going to believe this, but I have been chosen to receive the Presidential Citizens Medal at the White House." This is the second-highest civilian award given by a president to an individual "who has performed exemplary deeds or services for his or her country or fellow citizens." Two weeks later, Janice called again, this time saying, "I'm able to invite ten people to the White House ceremony where I will receive the Presidential Citizens Medal, and I put you on my list." Flabbergasted, I somehow managed to reply that I was incredibly honored and would be there. Wild horses in the middle of Pennsylvania Avenue could not keep me away! Janice received the Presidential Citizens Medal from President Obama on February 15, 2013 for creating and sustaining the Women Embracing Abilities Now program that supports newly disabled women in their quest for a return to independence. It was a truly memorable ceremony where Janice was joined by other outstanding leaders to receive their medals.

Recognizing the impact of the Americans with Disabilities Act is of paramount importance. This law continues to open the doors for people of all ages experiencing disabilities. We, at the Department of Disabilities, created annual celebrations of the ADA on July 26, the date it was signed into law. Governor O'Malley attended most of the celebrations and usually made an announcement of a new initiative that would benefit people with disabilities.

I was fortunate to have two outstanding deputies while Secretary of MDOD. A deputy secretary carries the lion's share of the everyday work with little recognition. My longtime friend and colleague, Diane McComb, stayed from the previous administration and was deputy for several months. When she resigned, I recruited George Failla, a young lawyer working at the Maryland State Department of Education. George was one of the dedicated volunteers who spent a week each summer guiding the students at the Maryland Youth Leadership Forum.

He certainly had the skills and experience to lead MDOD's policy team, and he became our department's Deputy Secretary in January 2008.

We accomplished many positive changes during my time at the Department of Disabilities and left much unfinished. While I am proud of our achievements, it was the closure of Rosewood that brought Maryland a step closer to full inclusion for people with intellectual disabilities.

After serving seven years in the governor's cabinet, I retired. It was time to embark on a new stage in my life.

I was sworn in as Secretary of the Maryland Department of Disabilities in March 2007 and afterward posed for a photo with Governor Martin O'Malley (right) and Lt. Governor Anthony Brown (left).

I joined Janice Jackson at the White House when she received the Presidential Citizens medal in 2013.

No Sirens, Please!

I was over sixty by this time and in the homestretch of my work life. I'd long ago given up public walking but still accumulated daily steps by circling the inside of my house. Beginning in the bedroom, I ambled down the hall to the kitchen, laser-focused on every step as if it were my last. Mindfulness trumps carelessness. From the kitchen where family members knew not to drip liquids on my path of travel, I proceeded through the dining room, foyer, back down the hall and into the bedroom. Safe! Another sixty steps, safe again. I did this each morning before leaving for work and a few times in the evening.

Each morning my husband left around seven a.m. to catch his train to Washington, DC. I marvel at his ability to not "helicopter" around me despite my track record of frequent falls. Risk-taking female meets low-anxiety male, and it was obviously a match made in heaven.

Said spouse was long gone by the time I took my morning stroll on this particular day. I was nearly finished when my crutch found a tiny corner of the hall runner with no padding under it, and PLOP! I was down quicker than Paul Simon could sing "Slip, Slidin' Away." Convinced I could push myself up, I scooted on my butt a few feet to the stairs. Wrong. My sixty-year-old arms were not the champions of my youth that could push, pull, or lift me out of any predicament. Drat! Scanning the vicinity for another large, strong object, I scooted again, this time to the ottoman in the living room. Too high. My Goldilocks moment was interrupted by thoughts of the tub surround. More scooting through the bedroom and into the master bathroom. Unfortunately, this was also too high and awkward. This was getting old fast, and my slacks were now a bit dirty from all the scooting.

Next, I did what any clever old lady would do. I called 911. Not really an emergency, just "battleship down." Since I couldn't reach the deadbolt on the front door, I directed the EMTs to go into the backyard, climb up on the deck, and I'd open the bedroom door for them. More scooting. Sirens signaled their arrival, no doubt alarming whatever neighbors hadn't left for work. Note to self: next time, No Sirens! All went according to plan. Two strong and friendly EMTs helped me to my feet, watched while I sat in my wheelchair, and inquired whether I was injured. "No, I'm not hurt, just late for work." "Work?" Yes, indeed. They returned to the ambulance and watched as I walked down my ramp and got into my car. I waved and smiled as I drove away.

This whole scene may have been a first for them but not a last. History repeated itself several months later . . . without sirens.

24

Grandchildren Are the Best!

My retirement preceded my husband's by two months and the birth of our first grandchild by an additional two weeks. It was love at first sight the day Brian joined the world. We spent the next two months seeing this precious baby as often as we could and then offered to watch him full-time once our daughter, Becca, returned to work. She agreed, and for the next two and a half years, Brian spent every weekday with us. These were high-quality moments when we had the opportunity not only to experience the joy of cuddling and playing with him each day but also to help shape the person he will become and to witness his emerging personality and early learning. Some days were long and we were exhausted when he went home. In retrospect, though, the time flew by. Suddenly, he was gone, off to a day care/preschool program where he could play with other children. Socialization with his peers was something we could not offer him. For the next five months of freedom, we caught up on neglected projects and took a few trips.

Grandchild number two, Caroline, was born during this hiatus and we began caring for her when her mother returned to work. Realizing that Caroline would most certainly be the last grandchild we would watch daily caused me to savor every day with her. Each time I held her, I was acutely aware that she might even be the last baby I would ever hold. With advancing age and torn rotator cuffs in both shoulders, my upper-body strength is diminishing. One of my great regrets was that I could not independently get down on the floor to play with Caroline or her brother before her. What was once effortless with my own children seemed impossible with my "grands." Twice with each grandchild I asked Jim to help me get down and back up, and each time the kids and I were thrilled with our brief playtime together. Have I mentioned that Jim is the kindest and most empowering husband ever?

We provided care for Caroline for two and a half years until she, too, went off to the day care/preschool program. She was at her program for six months when the pandemic shutdown occurred. Her parents struggled to keep two children busy while working at home. By mid-June 2020 when the shutdown began to ease, Jim and I offered to watch both children for the summer. Nana and Grandpa's Day Care reopened. Planning and preparing activities, engaging the children seven hours each day, then cleaning up afterwards was exhausting, but we loved this unexpected time with them. In September, Brian began participating in online school daily, and Caroline continued being with us for another nine months.

Each grandchild still spends at least one afternoon per week with us following school or summer day camp. Sometimes I get choked up when thinking about my grands, their innocence, and our fun times together. I will hold these memories close to my heart for the remainder of my life, but what will they remember?

This was Mother's Day 2019 spent with the best daughter in the world, Becca, and my "grands", Brian and Caroline.

PART 5

REFLECTIONS

25

My Mother

In Chapter Two, I am critical of my mother and refer several times to us having a complicated relationship. Other places in this memoir, I express my appreciation for her. Although we did indeed have a complex relationship, I loved and respected my mom. There were points in time when we clashed, but many others when we were quite close. As a parent myself, I understand that all parents make mistakes but do the best they can.

My respect for both my parents emanated from their wise decision-making for me. My parents were always my biggest fans and wanted the best for me. I never doubted their love. As for the friction between my mother and me, I believe I understood even at a young age that I was not the easiest child to parent, given my experience of being thrust into an institutional living situation when I was still a toddler.

I have shed more than a few tears in writing about my mother. How awful it must have been for her to ride in the ambulance to the hospital with her very sick little girl, wait while they tested and diagnosed me, hear the dreaded verdict that her baby had polio, then ride home alone on public transportation. She cried and the other passengers grew silent knowing that something terrible had happened to this woman who boarded the bus in front of the hospital. While that day may have been the worst of her life, her despair continued when her only child had to live apart from her for fourteen months. How brave she was.

I'm an advocate of forgiveness and believe it is empowering for both parties in a struggling relationship. I forgave my mother for her role in our clashes when I was a child and teen and wish she was still alive to consult with me on this memoir.

> *"It's not an easy journey, to get to a place where you forgive people. But it is such a powerful place, because it frees you."*
>
> —*Tyler Perry*

A Pat on the Head and Other Stereotypical Transgressions

In a world where women are still judged by their appearances, disabled women are often viewed in a much different way. Frequently, we run smack-dab into some of the following stereotypes.

Disabled Woman as a Perpetual Child

Perhaps I should be grateful to have made it into my thirties before anyone patted me on the head, a common experience of people with disabilities. The actual intrusion into my personal space was certainly shocking, but the perpetrator, witnesses, and scene of the crime were even more disturbing.

Here I was, a successful professional who had been asked by a prominent colleague to serve on a regional advisory committee. Normally after a meeting, I would go home, but this meeting was in a different state. Following the meeting came the social hour. I entered on foot, using my crutches. My colleague began with a round of introductions. When she got to her husband, he smiled and patted me on the head. It was not a tap, tap, tap sort of patting.

He brazenly stroked the back of my head as he said, "sweet." OMG! Did this stranger actually touch me? Although I wanted to growl and smack his hand, discretion was in order. And so, I remained silent.

Disabled Woman as an Invalid

As I gazed in the mirror, I was surprised to see I looked gorgeous that night, but you'll have to take my somewhat biased word for it. All decked out in a sparkly, two-piece dress with glittery stockings and silver shoes considered fashionable in the late '60s, I was ready for New Year's Eve with my new fiancé. I was excited. Prior to the main party at a hotel, there was a cocktail hour at the home of one of his high school classmates. We parked and walked across the street. Other partygoers were arriving and exchanging pleasantries. Outside and literally hanging on the railing with one arm while grasping a wine glass in her free hand was the classmate's mother. From the looks of it, she had been drinking for . . . a while. "Ahhhh," she said loudly as we climbed the steps, "I didn't know we were having an *invalid* at the party tonight." I never heard what she said after that. I was devastated.

Disabled Woman as Asexual

Our next-door neighbor was an older man who was an avid gardener always willing to offer advice to my husband, born and raised in New York City and still learning best practices for growing vegetables. By the time we moved to this neighborhood, we already had two children. We had lived there for over two years when he sprung this question on my husband, "Did you marry your wife after she was handicapped?" My husband assured him that I was indeed disabled when we met, married, and had children. Sigh.

Disabled Woman as Asexual, a Reprise

It was my freshman year in college. A male friend shared with me that one of his housemates was going to ask me out. This housemate was handsome and presented as polite and nice. I was intrigued. When the big approach and ask didn't happen within a month, I mentioned it to the guy who told me it was to occur. After some badgering on my part, he explained that their resident advisor, a senior, had laughingly told the young man who wanted to ask me out, "Just be sure you don't take along a magnet." Yeah, old Metal Mary here became a joke among this group of freshman guys. Another sigh.

26

What's Your Comfort Level?

Many people continue to be uncomfortable with disability despite our increased visibility and inclusion. Whether discomfort comes from lack of interaction with us, transference of attitudes from one's parents, cultural stereotypes that never seem to disappear, or feelings of fear, pity, or helplessness is unknown. Whatever the cause, like many other people with disabilities, I recognize my responsibility to educate and put people at ease.

My rule of thumb is that my mere presence and participation in various activities coupled with a friendly smile should be a sufficient statement about my capability for adults. I actively engage with children and youth, however.

March is Read Across America month and Governor O'Malley encouraged his cabinet members to schedule time to read at our local schools. This was a delightful opportunity to interact with young elementary school students. I found two books featuring children with disabilities that resonated with early elementary students and went to a few schools in my county each year as a guest reader. The kids enjoyed the stories, and many had questions that produced conversations.

When my son was about nine, his neighborhood friends stayed for lunch one Saturday. I happened to be out shopping that day, and my husband prepared and hosted the feast for this lunch bunch. One boy, who was a year older than my son, lingered in the kitchen and asked my husband about my disability. What seemed to be most pressing on his mind was the permanence of it. He asked, "Will Ms. Cathy ever recover?" Jim explained that I would not but could do most everything I wanted to do and gave this nine-year-old a brief explanation of adaptive strategies. When Jim relayed this conversation to me, I was struck by the ongoing nature of disability versus the world of cartoons kids watch. Cartoon characters fall off cliffs, run into brick walls, and are mangled by cars and trucks, yet within seconds are restored to their previous functioning. The permanence of disability can be unsettling to kids, particularly sensitive kids. Jim's quick analysis of the boy's question and explanation of adaptations were perfect.

After I retired, I volunteered at an afterschool homework club. On my first day there, I noticed a boy across the room staring at the undercarriage of my power chair. I smiled and gave him a little wave. Embarrassed, he quickly looked away. I busied myself with another child, and a few minutes later the boy from across the room was standing at my side. He kneeled to look at my chair. I said, "I'm a Transformer. Would you like to see how I do it?" He grinned and said, "Yes." With that, I began to show him and a growing group of children the various features of my power chair. I raised up two feet, returned to original height, tilted forward to pick up a pencil from the floor, then tilted the seat backwards to a forty-five-degree angle. By this time, all the budding engineers were down on the floor, watching what happened under the chair as I took it through its maneuvers. One girl, not particularly interested in the mechanics of my chair, began telling me about her grandmother who used a wheelchair. That led to a discussion of how beneficial a wheelchair can be. The children loved my power wheelchair and never seemed to tire of asking me to show them its various features.

Over the years, I occasionally attended work-related social events and at some observed a blind person standing by themselves. No one in the room may have known this blind individual, but these were gatherings of people who either experienced a disability or were professionals in the field. If those of us who promote acceptance of disabled people are uncomfortable with approaching a blind person at a social event, how can we expect members of the general public to be comfortable?

During my lifetime, the acceptance and inclusion of people with disabilities has improved markedly, yet there is still much to be accomplished. I encourage you to look for opportunities to promote understanding and inclusion.

27

An Awesome Life

My phone rang as I was approaching the guard station outside the White House gate on my way to the award ceremony where my friend Janice Jackson would receive her Citizen's Medal from President Obama. My daughter Becca was calling with an unrelated question. "Where are you?" she asked, recognizing that I was seldom in my office. I shared my destination. "You have the most awesome life," she replied.

Becca's remark has resurfaced in my mind many times since that day, and she was correct. My life, shaped by having polio so many years ago, has indeed been awesome.

Recognizing how my life was but a moment in time, I wanted to make a difference for people with disabilities. As I embarked on a journey to enhance the quality of life for all people with disabilities, it quickly became my mission. By joining with others who had a similar purpose and a vision of a future where all people are valued and included,

I know I made a difference. Together we laid the groundwork in Maryland that others continue to build upon.

In my personal life, my dreams were unspoken. A long and happy marriage, a fulfilling career, the chance to raise wonderful children, and to live long enough to not only see grandchildren, but to nurture them and contribute to their lives sometimes seemed like more than I deserved. Yet it happened.

Yes, I have fallen many times in my life, sometimes literally and often figuratively. I have broken bones but mostly just shattered my dignity. In reflecting on my life, perhaps my greatest fall was when I fell in love with Jim Raggio!

Baseball legend, Lou Gehrig said upon his retirement due to ALS, "*Today I consider myself the luckiest man on the face of the earth.*" Similarly, I have been incredibly lucky and will be forever grateful. I have realized my dreams and accomplished more than I ever thought possible.

Still in love with Jim!

With my strong and devoted son, Matthew.

Murphy's Laws of Falling

1. To a crutch user, a freshly painted wall is like a Siren beckoning to Ulysses.

2. If I nag my husband for a year to paint or touch up a wall, I will fall against it, leaving a big, ugly mark within one week after the paint job is complete.

3. Falls nearly always occur in front of spectators, rarely in private.

4. If a fall does occur in private, there is never a piece of furniture nearby that can be used to hoist oneself up.

5. If there is a quarter-inch wet spot on a 3,000-square-foot floor, my crutch will find it and down I go!

6. Throw rugs were invented by the Marquis de Sade to torture crutch users.

7. When I fall in public, the first person to my rescue is always a ninety-five-pound woman—God bless her.

8. Dust bunnies always find their way under crutches even if they must travel across the room to get there.

9. Slippery floors seldom look that way.

10. Fast food restaurants never dilute the cleanser used on their floors. Not only is it undiluted, they never bother to rinse it, so that there is always a slippery residue in place.

11. Freezing rain always falls on days when I have somewhere important to go.

12. You can tell the house inhabited by the person with the physical disability because it is the last to shovel the snow.

13. If there is one patch of ice remaining in the mall parking lot, it will be situated by the driver's side door of the only available parking space.

14. When the snowplow driver decides where to push the accumulated white stuff, he aims for the biggest parking space—the accessible ones, of course, because surely those folks don't venture out in bad weather, do they?

Acknowledgements

I will begin by thanking my editor, Elizabeth Ridley, for her comments and edits that were enormously helpful. I also appreciated Sheri Thomas sharing her publishing experience with me and connecting me with Patricia Marshall and her outstanding team at Luminare Press. Special thanks to my friend, Margaret Ann Nolan, who volunteered to proof the final document. Her keen eye was valuable and impressive.

The earliest reader of material within this memoir was my dear friend, Kimberly Riddle. She read, commented, and maintained custody of my essays. Decades later when I could not locate one of the essays, she proudly produced copies of the entire batch. Kim's support throughout the memoir writing process refreshed my resolve to finish telling the story.

I shared the opening chapter with my friend Mindy Morrell, another former Developmental Disabilities Council Director. She excitedly responded that she wanted to read more, and her excitement encouraged me to forge on. Mindy's comments on the first section provided valuable guidance.

"Besties" are hard to find, and I have been incredibly fortunate to have been the beneficiary of true friendship by many women. Transitioning to a new school in the middle of first grade was easy thanks to Nancy Williamson Edmondson. We immediately connected, supported each other, and had a ton of fun during childhood and our difficult teen years. Many thanks to Nancy for her encouragement and to her husband Wayne for providing some of the photos herein.

My college friends are amazing women whose friendship I cherish. Nancy Strauss Boos, Glenanne Zeigenfuse Farley, Boby Cramer Huffard, Chris Gruss Ketz, and Nancy Geiger Smith are the "gal pals" with whom I have shared college experiences and reunion joy. I have been fortunate to enjoy enduring friendship and get togethers also with Carol Berry Shumaker and Polly Graybill Buchanan.

My former neighbors have become like family: Gail and David Foley, Margaret Ann Nolan and Mark Houck, Trish and Bob Hemler, Karen and Jim Trennepohl, Marianne O'Leary and Jon Traunfeld, and Phoebe Tobin and her late husband Bill. Some are also in our pinochle group, including Gail, Mark, Trish and Bob, Karen, the founder of the group, and Jim Trennepohl. Other pinochle group members include: the late Joan Harring and Jeff Harring and the "East Side Gang" from Baltimore County: the late Jack Nolan, Marlene Skipper, Susan and Dan Buehl and Mike McGraw. All have enriched my life tremendously!

Prior to my move to Maryland, I was fortunate to have an extraordinary mentor in the late Marshall Jacobson, Esq. who served as the President of the United Cerebral Palsy of Wyoming Valley Board of Directors when I was the Executive Director.

There are many former colleagues who I joined in advocating for more progressive disability services in Maryland. I will refrain from naming them because I inadvertently would overlook someone. Together we made some remarkable changes!

I will always be grateful to Phil Holmes, who hired me at the Maryland Developmental Disabilities Council. From the outset, Phil was an excellent mentor. In addition to Phil, I appreciate the many wonderful members of the DD Council who, as volunteers, devoted countless hours of their time to our meetings and my phone calls.

My heartfelt thanks goes to Cristine Marchand, former Executive Director of The Arc Maryland, who asked me to start and facilitate the self-advocacy group, People on the Go (POG). I am grateful also to the amazing members of POG for their friendship and for teaching me to really listen.

Starting a nonprofit organization could have resulted in failure were it not for the board members of Independence Now (IN). Original members included the late Bill Lee, Maggie Roffee, Marsha Mazz, Pat Laird, Kathleen Wolf, Bobby Bobo, Regina Lee, and Harold Krauthamer. Their dedication and creativity were truly remarkable!

I also want to acknowledge the three original staff at IN, Ross Silvers, Dori Spittel Tempio and Patricia Tate. It was touch and go at the beginning, but these three made us successful!

To Sarah Basehart: I cannot begin to tell you how much I appreciate your very fine leadership of my beloved organization, Independence Now. You have kept it strong, relevant, and growing.

My deep appreciation will always be with Governor Martin O'Malley for closing Rosewood, Maryland's oldest institution, and for giving me the opportunity to serve in his cabinet where I could pursue new initiatives and responsive public policy for people with disabilities.

Finally, to my husband Jim, daughter Becca, son Matt and their spouses Shel and Colin: I love you and very much appreciate your encouragement. To my "grands" Brian and Caroline: thank you for being your darling and entertaining selves.

Made in the USA
Middletown, DE
03 September 2024

60272622R00130